PASSENGER TRAINS
IN THE NORTH OF ENGLAND

PASSENGER TRAINS
IN THE NORTH OF ENGLAND

1957-2022

JOHN MATTHEWS

PEN & SWORD
TRANSPORT

AN IMPRINT OF PEN & SWORD BOOKS LTD.
YORKSHIRE – PHILADELPHIA

First published in Great Britain in 2023 by
Pen and Sword Transport
An imprint of
Pen & Sword Books Ltd
Yorkshire - Philadelphia

ISBN 978 1 39909 480 1

Typeset in Palatino 10/12 by SJmagic DESIGN SERVICES, India.

Printed and bound in the UK by CPI Group (UK) Ltd., Croydon. CR0 4YY.

Pen & Sword Books Ltd incorporates the Imprints of Pen & Sword Books Archaeology, Atlas, Aviation, Battleground, Discovery, Family History, History, Maritime, Military, Naval, Politics, Railways, Select, Transport, True Crime, Fiction, Frontline Books, Leo Cooper, Praetorian Press, Seaforth Publishing, Wharncliffe and White Owl.

For a complete list of Pen & Sword titles please contact

PEN & SWORD BOOKS LIMITED
47 Church Street, Barnsley, South Yorkshire, S70 2AS, England
E-mail: enquiries@pen-and-sword.co.uk
Website: www.pen-and-sword.co.uk

or

PEN AND SWORD BOOKS
1950 Lawrence Rd, Havertown, PA 19083, USA
E-mail: Uspen-and-sword@casematepublishers.com
Website: www.penandswordbooks.com

FSC
www.fsc.org

MIX
Paper | Supporting
responsible forestry
FSC® C013604

CONTENTS

INTRODUCTION

With over two years in the writing and numerous setbacks due to the pandemic, *Freight Trains in the North of England* finally appeared on the bookshelves in 2021. Following on from that it seemed a good idea to start work on a new companion book, *Passenger Trains in the North of England*, for publication in 2023. Writing an Introduction to the book has proved quite a problem with the ever changing fortunes of our railways, especially when you take into account the problems of the Covid pandemic and serious industrial relations issues. At the time of writing this Introduction in Spring 2023, the passenger train network is still seeing continued disruption to train services as the frustrated traveller contends with strikes, delays, cancellations and increased fares. Hopefully by the time you read this, peace will have broken out and passengers will be getting the train service they need and deserve. Moving on, the environmental advantages of the railways cannot be over emphasised, and as the country and the wider world try to deal with the serious issues of climate change, railways will become more vital than ever. So, while our railways have an exciting future ahead, this book takes a look back at the last sixty years and captures the great number and variety of passenger trains that have run on the railways of the North of England.

The format for this book is similar to the earlier one, although the section on Nottingham has been replaced by the opening chapter on Cheshire. The photographs are from the very best railway photographers working with their film cameras in both industrial and beautiful landscape settings. While the odd recent digital image has found its way into the book, the majority have been taken with Pentax 67, Mamiya 645 and earlier 35mm cameras using a variety of black and white film like Ilford FP4 and HP5. Pictures capturing the huge diversity of trains, locomotives and locations add up to produce a book that takes a detailed look at many of the passenger trains of the North of England. It goes without saying that to try to cover the complete history of Northern passenger trains would be nigh on impossible. The great collection of pictures included are just a reminder of the times we knew and will hopefully take the reader back to what were perhaps happier and less chaotic times. While doing research for this book I discovered that the first passenger train was in fact run by the Swansea and Mumbles Railway at Oystermouth in 1807 using horse drawn wagons. A little later, in September 1825, the first locomotive hauled public railway opened between Stockton and Darlington using Stephenson's *Locomotion No.1*. This in turn led to the first Inter-City train operated between Liverpool and Manchester in 1830. The decline in passenger numbers in the early 1920s, due to competition from new roads and increased private car ownership, led to virtually all rail companies being grouped into the 'Big Four' of Great Western, London North Eastern, London Midland

Scottish and Southern railways on 1 January 1923.

The next big change came on the 1 January 1948 when the railways were nationalised to become British Railways. Initially there was an increase in passengers using the trains and the network became profitable. This was not maintained and big losses were encountered in the 1950s and early 1960s leading to the Beeching Report, 'The Reshaping of British Railways (1963)', which axed many branch and secondary lines. The closure of a large number of freight depots also led to the transfer of huge amounts of traffic on to the new motorways being built, not a coincidence in many people's view! The introduction of InterCity and HST trains in the late 1970s brought passengers back to the railways and resulted in it becoming profitable again.

Between the years 1994 and 1997 British Rail, as it was known by then, was privatised and the passenger services franchised to originally twenty-five private companies and the freight sector sold off. While the franchise system has been heavily criticised, passenger numbers did increase at a good rate and in fact by 2014 they were at their highest ever levels. All appeared to be rosy until March 2020 when dark clouds gathered and the pandemic brought not only big problems for the railways but tragedy and loss of life for an untold number of people in this country and around the world. In late July 2020 it was announced that the railway network was as good as nationalised again with virtually all the train companies now part of the public sector and that since March 2020, the Department for Transport has spent a large amount of taxpayers' money to keep the trains running. Ironically in January 2020 the Government launched its 'Restore Your Railway' scheme, which aims to bring back lines, stations and services that were lost under the Beeching cuts.

In the pages that follow we will journey north to the Scottish Borders highlighting a great variety of trains along the way, including main line expresses, branch line services, special charters, rail tours and many more. A good mix of steam, diesel and electric workings will hopefully stir memories of some of your favourite journeys of the past through the northern hills and industrial towns. Long forgotten passenger services and now closed lines will also feature, along with the stations, signals and other atmospheric scenes of days gone by.

John Matthews
June 2023

ACKNOWLEDGEMENTS

Restoration and Archiving Trust.

I would like to dedicate this book to William and Charles.

CHESHIRE

The county of Cheshire is a mainly rural area bordering the large industrial conurbations of Merseyside and Greater Manchester. The county's railways date back over 180 years to when both the Chester to Birkenhead and Chester to Crewe lines were opened in the autumn of 1840. The Cheshire Lines Committee was formed in the early 1860s and its 143 miles of railway served Manchester, Northwich, Winsford, Knutsford and Southport amongst many others. Although a large agricultural area, Cheshire does have a good number of long-standing industries including chemicals, salt, aerospace and Bentley cars. Born in the county in 1832 was author Lewis Carroll, famous for his book *Alice's Adventures in Wonderland* and the popularisation of the fictional Cheshire Cat. Last but not least is Cheshire's world-famous dairy product, its crumbly cheese, the UK's largest seller.

We start our journey with a view of the *Pines Express* arriving at Crewe on 29 April 1961. Setting out from Manchester, the service would travel through to Bournemouth, including the Somerset and Dorset line along the way. First run in 1910, it wasn't until 1927 that it gained its official *Pines Express* title. Jointly operated by the Midland Railway and the LNWR, the train last ran in March 1967, although its final trip along the S&DJR was in September 1962. In the early days of main line electric haulage, two 25kV a.c. locos, Nos. E3304 and E3036, bring the service towards Crewe Station. (John S. Whiteley)

Pausing at Crewe on 29 April 1961 is the Up *Mid-Day Scot* to London Euston headed by English Electric Type 4 No. D 319. Introduced by the LMS Railway in 1927 the train started out from Edinburgh Princes Street and Glasgow Central before joining up and heading south for the capital. By 1960, the *Mid-Day Scot* was completing the full journey in seven hours and fifteen minutes with only a single stop at Carlisle. (John S. Whiteley)

While electric and diesel engines were becoming more common, steam could still be seen in good numbers, and on 23 June 1962 Stanier 4-6-0 No. 45180 starts off from Crewe with a train to Blackpool. Built in 1935, the Black Five was withdrawn from 5B Crewe South shed in September 1965 having previously spent some time at Saltley. (John S. Whiteley)

Crossing the WCML near Moore just south of Warrington, former LNER B1 No. 61050 is running west with the 10.00 SO Sheffield to Llandudno train on 31 August 1963. Designed by Thompson and classed as 5MT locos, these fine 4-6-0 engines were introduced from 1942 and gave excellent service well into the 1960s. (PJF Collection)

A dramatic image at Warrington as one of the BR Standard 7P6F Britannia locomotives powers a southbound express towards the bridge over the Manchester Ship Canal. The 4-6-2 Pacific, of which there were fifty-five in the class, can be seen on 17 September 1966. (G. Dixon)

At Chester we catch a view of No. 44717 arriving from Shrewsbury with a Paddington to Birkenhead service on 5 January 1967. The Stanier 4-6-0 would soon be removed from the working, allowing Standard 4 No. 76095 to complete the run through to its final destination in the Wirral Merseyside, which until 1974 was in the county of Cheshire. (Peter Fitton)

On 5 March 1967, an SLS special ran to bid farewell to the GWR Birmingham to Birkenhead service. Starting out from Tyseley behind No. 7029, the train ran via Shrewsbury and Ruabon and later returned to Birmingham Snow Hill with No. 44680 in charge. In between, Standard 9F loco No. 92234 took the tour on a return trip from Birkenhead to Chester via Hooton, where it is seen here. A second special also ran that day using the same engines but in reverse order, while No. 92203 took over for the run to Chester and back. (Gavin Morrison)

Pictured arriving at Crewe on 29 January 1977 is the *Western Memorial Railtour* organised by Railway Pictorial Publications. The special departed Paddington at 08.20 and then travelled north to Cheshire via Bristol and Hereford. Western hydraulic loco No. D1023 *Western Fusilier* brings the train past the Mornflake Oats Gresty Road Mill; the company has been a resident of Crewe for nearly 350 years. Recently the firm extended its sponsorship at Crewe Alexandra FC by naming their ground the Mornflake Stadium. (Peter Fitton)

For a number of years Class 25 Bo-Bo diesels were regular performers on the Cardiff Central workings and here on 16 June 1979 No. 25245 sets off with the 13.45 from Crewe. The lightweight load of just four coaches would cause few problems for the Sulzer six cylinder 1,250bhp loco. (Martin Hilbert)

Departing Chester on the return leg of a special from Hull is preserved Class 5 No. 5305. The former LMS Stanier 4-6-0 passes the impressive Chester No.2 signal box that controlled the east end of the station and the junction lines to Manchester and Crewe. For a time in the mid-1960s, No. 45305, as it was numbered then, was in fact allocated to the nearby Chester 6A shed. Ironically, on this day, 18 April 1981, the Black Five was returning to the place from which it was rescued after the end of main line steam. At Albert Drapers of Hull No. 45305 was the last steam engine on the scrap line, and just before the cutters' torches got to work it was fortunately reprieved by the scrapyard owner and returned to steam again in 1976. (John S. Whiteley)

Replacing the earlier Class 25s, a few years later BRC&W Type 3 engines could be seen working at Crewe. These Sulzer powered locos were introduced from 1960 onwards producing 1,550 bhp and weighing just over 73 tons. On a bright 10 October 1983, No. 33039 sets off with the 16.06 to Cardiff Central. Originally numbered D6557 and built in 1961, it was based at both Hither Green and Eastleigh during its twenty-eight years on the main line. (John S. Whiteley)

The railway from Skelton Junction to Warrington lost its passenger service in the 1960s but continued to see considerable freight traffic until final closure of the route on 7 July 1985. A year and a half earlier, Hertfordshire Railtours had run a special from St. Pancras to Amlwch on Anglesey, and here the *Britannia Belle* is seen crossing the Manchester Ship Canal at Latchford with No. 45111 *Grenadier Guardsman* leading the way. Two other locos were also used on the middle sections of the tour, Nos. 47537 and 40122, before the Peak took the train back to the capital. (Paul Shannon)

Port Sunlight centenary celebrations took place at the beginning of May 1988. Included in the festivities was the running of a number of special trains by the Wirral Transport Users Association. On 1 May, GWR No. 4566 picks its way through the long grass with a Lubrizol Junction to Port Sunlight train. Helping out on the special trains was LMS No. 7298 which was on the rear. (Peter Fitton)

Lying on the south bank of the River Mersey, Runcorn is the location here as a Euston to Liverpool Lime Street Inter-City service heads north on 4 September 1995. At the front is No. 90013 *The Law Society*, built at Crewe in November 1988, and after many years working along the West Coast Main Line it was transferred to East Anglia and later onto Freightliner. (Paul Shannon)

Once a major hub in the Speedlink wagonload network, Walton Old Junction Yard is the location of this image on 13 February 1991. Arriving from the south is single unit dmu No. 01, this driver training special is passing through the busy junction that today is mainly used for wagon storage. (John Matthews)

The small village of Bunbury is situated south of Tarporley on the Shropshire Union Canal. In this wintry scene near the village on 30 December 2000, loco No. 37429 is heading the 08.50 Holyhead to Wolverhampton train. This was possibly the last day of loco-haulage on this particular working. The English Electric Type 3 first appeared in August 1965 and was allocated to Cardiff Canton as No. D6600. (Peter Fitton)

At Chester on 24 March 2004, EWS loco No.47750, still in Virgin colours, heads the First North-Western 13.16 Bangor to Crewe train. Problems with the Class 175 Coradias had seen the reintroduction of North Wales loco-hauled services using First Great Western Mk. 2 coaches. Entering traffic on 6 March 1965 and carrying the number D1667, the Brush Type 4 was named *Atlas* at Cardiff in June 1966. (Martin Hilbert)

Departing north from Warrington Bank Quay on 9 June 2019 is A1A-A1A No 31128 *Charybdis* with the Branch Line Society's *Sunday Yicker* rail tour. After taking in various goods lines around Crewe, the train ran to Wigan and then onto the Haydock Branch that had re-opened for stone trains in October 2018. The special was top and tailed throughout, with No. 37668 sharing the workload on the lightweight four-coach special. (John Matthews)

Since the closure of Fiddlers Ferry Power Station in March 2020, the line from Latchford to Ditton has seen very limited use with only the occasional freight train using the route. On Grand National Day 9 April 2022, it came in handy, though, when loco No. 67014 brought the empty stock of a race day special from Runcorn to Arpley Sidings Warrington, photographed passing Crosfields. (John Matthews)

DERBYSHIRE

Located in the East Midlands, the county has within its boundaries the picturesque Peak District National Park and the southern Pennines, making its rolling hills and uplands a mecca for ramblers and tourists alike. The Midland Railway chose Derby for its headquarters and the first station opened in 1839. Lying 127 miles from St. Pancras, Derby was included in many early railway projects to link the city with Sheffield, Bristol, Nottingham and London. Today the station, an important point on the Midland Main Line from London to Leeds, is also served by long-distance Cross-Country services from Scotland to Penzance and Bournemouth plus local trains to Matlock, Newark and Crewe.

At Crowden on 18 April 1964, EM2 Class No. 27002 *Aurora* is running eastbound on the 08.30 Manchester Piccadilly to Sheffield Victoria service. Built at Gorton in Manchester, the seven 1,500 V. d.c. locos were named after characters from Greek mythology. They appeared on the Woodhead route from 1954 and ran until their mass withdrawal and export to Dutch national railways in September 1969. (Peter Fitton)

Coming towards the end of its near thirty years on the main line, Jubilee 4-6-0 No. 45705 *Seahorse* heads the LCGB *High Peak Rail Tour* up the 1 in 90 at Chinley North on 18 September 1965. Built in May 1936, it had taken over the special from No. 4472 at Cheadle Heath, before running to Derby and finally London Paddington. (Peter Fitton)

Early February 1968 produced a covering of snow accompanied by sunshine in the Peak District, and on 3 February Sulzer type 4 No. D29 (later No. 45002) is approaching Chapel-en-le-Frith Central station which was to close about one month later. It is heading a Manchester to St. Pancras express and is working wrong line due to engineering work in Dove Holes Tunnel. Class 8F 2-8-0 No. 48117 is standing in the siding before setting back on to the main line with a freight from Gowhole Yard to Buxton. (John S. Whiteley)

A total of 852 Stanier designed Class 8F 2-8-0s were built between 1935 and 1946 at a variety of locations including Crewe, Horwich, Swindon and Eastleigh Works. Although principally used on heavy goods trains, they did occasionally appear on passenger workings, and of the fourteen that survived, both Nos. 48151 and 48773 have run on the main line while in preservation. At Hathersage on 20 March 1968, No. 48374 takes water en route to Earles Sidings after turning at Dore. (Les Nixon)

The *North West Tour* special ran on 20 April 1968, starting out from Birmingham New Street and then taking in a number of lines in Lancashire and Derbyshire. Jointly organised by the Manchester Rail Travel and Severn Valley Railway societies, a variety of locomotives were used on the day, including Nos. 73134, 73069, 48773, 92160 and a pair of Black Fives, Nos. 45110 and 44949. The Stanier 4-6-0s are pictured here heading north at Great Rocks during their run from Stockport to Stalybridge. (Gavin Morrison)

A little over a week before the end of regular passenger trains on the Woodhead route, No. 6723 catches the low winter sun while heading a Manchester-Harwich train at Valehouse. Photographed on 27 December 1969, it was re-numbered 37023 in March 1974. The EE Type 3, first based at March in July 1961, then went on to spend time at Stratford, Healey Mills and Motherwell. It is now undergoing restoration at the Pontypool and Blaenavon Railway. (Peter Fitton)

Staying on the Woodhead line we can now see the *Peaks Express* rail tour of 15 October 1977. This special ran from St. Pancras to Manchester Piccadilly and was pulled by three different 1Co-Co1 engines, Nos. 44002 *Helvellyn*, 44007 *Ingleborough* and here 44004 *Great Gable* heading west at Torside. New to service in 1959, the ten Sulzer powered locos, built at Derby, were originally numbered D1 to 10. Initially used on WCML expresses, two members of the class, D4 and D8, found their way into preservation. (Les Nixon)

Manufactured at Doncaster and originally numbered in the series 26000 to 26057, the EM1 class 1,500 V. d.c. locos operated on the Woodhead route until its closure in 1981. On 16 September 1978, Nos. 76028 and 76025 bring the Thompson B1 Locomotive Society's *Three Way Special* westbound over Broadbottom Viaduct heading for Manchester Piccadilly. The 41 meter high viaduct spans the River Etherow between Derbyshire and Greater Manchester. Starting off from London Marylebone behind a pair of Class 25s, No. 40186 then powered the train between Nuneaton and Rotherwood from where the electrics took over. By this time specials were the only passenger workings on the line. (Peter Fitton)

Departing Chesterfield on 5 May 1979 is No. 45111 *Grenadier Guardsman* with a St. Pancras to Sheffield service. Looking beyond the scrapyard to the right is the Parish Church of St. Mary and All Saints commonly known as the Crooked Spire. The largest church in Derbyshire, dating back to the fourteenth century, it is a Grade 1 listed building with its leaning twisted spire measuring 228 feet above the ground. (Gavin Morrison)

A four car dmu comprising Class 123 power car E52092, Class 124 trailer E59765, Class 123 trailer E59823 and Class 123 power car E52105 passes Edale on an eastbound working on 26 March 1981. Mixed formations of Classes 123 and 124 were common at that time after the Class 123s moved north to join the Class 124 Trans-Pennine fleet. Edale signal box, dating back to 1893, was still operational in 2021. (Paul Shannon)

Located in the Peak District, around ten miles south-west of Sheffield, is the village of Hathersage. Nearby, in December 1985, a Class 31 loco runs westbound along the Hope Valley line with a Hull to Manchester working. (Les Nixon)

Passing through New Mills South Junction on 31 January 1987 is the 07.20 Blackpool North to Harwich Parkeston Quay train led by Brush loco No. 47608. Built at Crewe, it first ran in August 1965 when numbered D1962, but after receiving a further four numbers and the name *Captain Peter Manisty RN* it was scrapped at Wigan in October 2000. Long distance trains like these, covering a number of secondary routes, are virtually a thing of the past and today anyone wishing to undertake this journey would have to change four times and travel via London on the average six-hour journey! Progress? I think not. (John Matthews)

Class 50 Co-Co engine No. 50012 *Benbow* approaches Great Rocks Junction on the freight-only line between Chinley and Buxton. The Hertfordshire Railtours *Derbyshire Dingle* special from London Paddington ran on a very wintry 8 February 1986. In addition to 50012, Nos. 50016 *Barham* and 45022 *Lytham St. Annes* also headed parts of the tour to Manchester Piccadilly and back. (Paul Shannon)

On 12 March 1987 the 08.45 Liverpool Lime Street to Sheffield train is pictured at a snowy Chinley led by loco No. 31450. Numbered from 31400 to 31469, the 31/4 class of locomotives were conversions of the earlier 31/1s with ETH fitted. Built by Brush Traction between 1957 and 1962, a total of 263 were originally turned out with Mirrlees 1,250bhp engines but when these proved unsuccessful the whole class was re-engined with English Electric 1,470bhp units between 1965 and 1969. (John Matthews)

At Ollerbrook, just to the east of Edale, HST power car No. 43089 brings up the rear of the diverted 09.00 St. Pancras to Manchester Piccadilly working. Initially sent to Heaton depot Newcastle in May 1978, 43089 was formed in HST set No. 254017 and became a regular performer on the East Coast Main Line until electrification saw it transferred to Laira. After a number of further moves, it was donated to the '125 Group' by Porterbrook in August 2020. This picturesque view in the Peak District was captured on 27 January 2004. (Gavin Morrison)

SOUTH YORKSHIRE

Lying to the east of the Pennines, the metropolitan county of South Yorkshire consists of four boroughs, Rotherham, Barnsley, Doncaster and, the largest, Sheffield. Its renowned steel making industry developed thanks to locally mined deposits of coal and iron plus a plentiful supply of water from nearby rivers that ran down off the Pennines. The three major rivers in the area are the Dearne, Rother and Don. As early as 1845 railways were being promoted with the initial aim of moving coal. The South Yorkshire Railway (SYR) was one of the most prominent and after a period called the SYR and River Don Company, it became part of the Manchester, Sheffield and Lincolnshire Railway in 1864. The county's busy rail network today sees a great selection of LNER, Cross County, Trans-Pennine and local services.

Arrived at Penistone on 9 May 1959 is one of the very last Class C14s, No. 67445. Built by Beyer, Peacock in 1907, the 4-4-2T, previously numbered LNER 6125 and 7445, was in operation until the final day of 1959 when it was withdrawn from Barnsley 36D shed. On this day it is taking water having just worked an all-stations service from Barnsley. (Gavin Morrison)

An impressive line-up at Sheffield Midland in September 1961. Viewed left to right are Ivatt 2-6-0 No. 46400, 'Royal Scot' No. 46137 *The Prince of Wales's Volunteers (South Lancashire)* on a southbound express and Stanier Black Five No. 44849 with a local train to Chinley. All three locos would continue to work on the main line for a number of years with the Ivatt Class 2 being the last in service in May 1967. (Peter Fitton)

Saturday 15 June 1963 marked the end of steam hauled expresses on the East Coast Main Line to London, after which they were to be diesel hauled. In fact, steam engines were officially barred from running into King's Cross station, except in emergencies. In this view at Doncaster, Gresley A4 No. 60006 *Sir Ralph Wedgwood* and the Anglo-Scottish Car Carrier take a short rest during a crew change. (Peter Fitton)

After steam was eliminated from King's Cross Station in June 1963, certain ECML trains were still to be seen behind steam engines, particularly in Yorkshire. On 3 August, A4 No. 60034 *Lord Faringdon* was photographed while stopped in Doncaster No. 8 platform on a Newcastle express after replacing a failed diesel further south. The loco had been transferred from 34A Top Shed to 34E New England Peterborough, and was later moved to Scotland to work the Glasgow to Aberdeen three-hour expresses. (Peter Fitton)

In the early evening sun Stanier Class 5 No. 45073 departs Sheffield Midland with the 17.30 to Manchester Piccadilly in September 1965. Local workings down the Hope Valley were among the very last steam hauled trains out of Sheffield Midland. The photographer remembers this train well, as it was his regular commute home to Grindleford and almost certain to be a Black Five. The morning service, Les recalls, was often hauled by an Ivatt 2-6-0 from Buxton shed with Nos. 46465 and 46401 both regular performers. (Les Nixon)

In July 1966 'Jubilee' Class No. 45643 *Rodney* runs towards Barnsley Exchange with a Bradford to Weymouth Saturday Only special. The train is coming down the bank from the nearby Summer Lane station which was on the line from Penistone and joining the railway running in from Wakefield Westgate. At one time Exchange station only had the one platform serving trains from Wakefield, but this changed when the nearby Court House station closed and a second platform was added. The new platform was built on the site of the old 36D steam shed. (Les Nixon)

South of Doncaster station at Black Carr, English Electric powered No. 259 is seen with a Saturdays Only Newcastle to Yarmouth service. A total of 200 Class 40 locos were built between 1958 and 1962, and by the time of this picture, 4 August 1973, the still operational 199 engines were all based at depots in the north of England or Scotland. Ill-fated Type 4 No. D322 had been condemned in May 1966 after a serious accident at Acton Grange Junction. (Peter Fitton)

Running through the closed Sheffield Victoria station on a bright 4 December 1976 are Sulzer Bo-Bo locos Nos. 24082 and 24087. The *Great Central* rail tour was organised by the Wirral Railway Circle and took in the Woodhead route on its trip from Crewe to Loughborough. Originally numbered D5100 to D5150 and built between 1958 and 1961, the final Class 24 to be withdrawn in October 1980 was No. 24081, finding its way into preservation at the Gloucestershire & Warwickshire Railway. (Gavin Morrison)

The same rail tour but viewed from a completely different angle. Nearing Penistone, the special encounters a pair of Class 76 electrics numbered 76010 and 76016, these are travelling westbound with a train of coal hoppers, probably for Fiddlers Ferry power station after an engine change at Guide Bridge. (Peter Fitton)

Passing through a very wet Masboro Station South Junction on 12 February 1977 is the F&W Tours *Western Finale*. After a 6.30 am start from Exeter St. Davids, the special train journeyed north via Birmingham and Derby to reach York at 1.07 pm. Class 52 No. D1023 *Western Fusilier*, built at Swindon in September 1963, is in charge of the working, and after withdrawal in February 1977, travelled to York once again to be part of the collection at the National Railway Museum. (Peter Fitton)

Black Carr Junction is about two miles south east of Doncaster on the once GNR main line to King's Cross where the joint GER/GNR tracks leave towards Lincoln. The South Yorkshire Joint Railway bridge once made a good place for photographing trains, and on Wednesday, 13 April 1977 Peter Fitton was there to record No. 55008 *The Green Howards* heading north with the 4pm King's Cross to Edinburgh 'Talisman'. Sadly, a year later, all the semaphores were to go when the area was re-signalled. (Peter Fitton)

On a very hot 18 June 1978, two Class 20-hauled 'Doncaster Detour' trains were run to Doncaster Railex 125 which celebrated 125 years of the 'Plant' railway works. Just after 5pm, Nos. 20186 and 20187 were photographed arriving with the 11-coach empty stock for the first return train, here seen from the North Bridge crossing the river on the approach to Doncaster station. Another pair of Type 1 locos numbered 20009 and 20064 worked the other special, both pairs running to Birmingham, where No. 50016 took over the first one while Nos. 31123 and 31163 headed the second back to Paddington. (Peter Fitton)

Against the backdrop of Hatfield Main Colliery, Deltic No. 55015 *Tulyar* is seen running towards Doncaster with the 09.33 Hull to King's Cross service. Located at Stainforth, the mine was opened in 1915, and although there were numerous owners over the years, including the National Coal Board in 1947, it carried on producing coal right through to its final closure in 2015. This was due to the lack of demand and increase in carbon taxes. (Les Nixon)

The Midland Railway signal box at Totley Tunnel East is seen from the adjacent footbridge, which was an excellent place for photographing passing trains. On 10 June 1988, No. 31446 and the 15.22 Sheffield to Manchester and Liverpool train are seen heading west towards Hope. Totley Tunnel, built by the Midland Railway, was opened in 1893 and ran for 6,230 yards (3.54m) between Totley on the outskirts of Sheffield and Grindleford in Derbyshire. (Peter Fitton)

Crossing Norfolk Bridge near Attercliffe, Sheffield on 23 August 2014 is No. 47815 *Great Western*. The Brush engine is on the rear of a Doncaster to Great Yarmouth special high above the River Don in its bright blue livery. Coming up to date, by January 2023 the two-tone green liveried loco was owned by the Rail Operations Group and listed as non-operational.

(Gavin Morrison)

NORTH-WEST

Before 1974 this part of the book would have fitted neatly under the heading of 'Lancashire', but major boundary changes transformed the County with the creation of Greater Manchester, Merseyside and the northern parts around Barrow and Cartmel moving into the newly formed Cumbria. In all over 700 square miles of land was lost from Lancashire to the new areas, around two-fifths in total.

The North-West today is a modern thriving region with industries including BAE, Rolls-Royce, the tourist trade and traditional names like Thwaites and Hollands turning out beer and pies respectively like they have done for over 100 years. Although coal mining and cotton making are now relegated to the past, they are still very much part of the area's history and the North-West's railways today owe much to these early industries. Proposals to reinstate the Colne to Skipton line, the Burscough Curves and a passenger service between Clitheroe and Hellifield are high on many agendas and would dramatically improve things for many travellers, if they come to pass.

The train pictured is the 09.05 from Manchester Victoria to Wakefield seen at Castleton station. Usually, this train was worked by a Normanton loco off the early morning Normanton to Victoria mail. However, the mail did not run on Bank Holidays, so this shot taken on August Bank Holiday Monday, 3 August 1960, shows the service headed by one of Newton Heath's Ivatt 2-6-0s, No. 46487, which were rarely seen on local passenger work. (Richard Greenwood)

The holiday and excursion traffic to Blackpool from the Sheffield and Chesterfield areas was significant. This was so particularly at the time of the Blackpool Illuminations. A Stanier Mogul No. 42971, as seen here on 11 September 1960, was distinctly unusual. The train is passing the Dunlop Cotton Mill, once the largest textile mill in Europe, and is approaching Castleton where at East Junction it will turn off the main line to Manchester Victoria in order to take the branch towards Bury and Bolton. (Richard Greenwood)

Bank Hall (Liverpool) had a small allocation of four British Railways Standard Class 2 locos that replaced former L&Y 2-4-2Ts. Until 1961 they worked turn and turnabout with LMS Class 2 4-4-0s on stopping trains such as the 3.50pm Rochdale to Wigan Wallgate. On 3 April 1961, No. 78043 is entering Knowsley Street station at Bury. To the left is a typical LMS warehouse and beyond can be seen some gantries for the goods yard cranes. The signal at the extreme right is on the connecting line from Bury Loco Junction to Bury Loop Junction. (Richard Greenwood)

Approaching Smithy Bridge on 23 December 1961 is an eastbound express from Liverpool Exchange behind loco No. 45698 *Mars*. The freight train waiting in the Down loop is the empty steel bolster working from Brewery Sidings (Manchester) to Tees Yard. At the head is an ex-LNER V2 No. 60877; a class of loco strictly banned from this route, but at least another six appearances were known about. (Richard Greenwood)

Around noon on a sunny 27 June 1961, English Electric Type 4 No. D319 is seen departing Preston with the southbound *Caledonian* running non-stop to London Euston. Diesels had taken over many of the West Coast main line expresses by this date, at least this one carried a headboard. The south bank, next to Preston No. 1 signal box (just over the old 'glass bridge' which connected the station to the former Park Hotel), was an excellent place for morning photographs in those busy and mostly steam days. (Peter Fitton)

On 29 January 1962 Liverpool were drawn to play Oldham Athletic in the Fourth Round of the FA Cup. Four excursion trains were scheduled to run to Oldham Werneth, the nearest station to the ground. They were all worked by ex-LMS Black Fives of which two had Caprotti valve gear. Of the four, only No. 44744 took on an assisting engine in the shape of an Ivatt 2-6-0, No. 46417 of Bury shed. The driver of 44744 must have had doubts about the gradients from Bury to Heywood and Rochdale to Shaw. This train is seen passing under the road bridge between Shaw and Newhey in the district of Shaw known as 'Goats'. (Richard Greenwood)

At Shaw station we see another of the football specials of 29 January 1962 heading for Oldham Werneth behind Caprotti valve engine number 44742. (Richard Greenwood)

In June 1962, CWS Manchester organised a week-long holiday at Scarborough. The special train had twelve passenger coaches and a luggage van. Outwards the London Midland Region provided a 'Royal Scot' to head the train, but for the return a week later, the Eastern Region were no more imaginative than to find an 8F 2-8-0, No. 48123. This was a disappointment to local enthusiasts waiting to photograph it at Summit West on 11 June. (Richard Greenwood)

In the early 1960s a favourite place for train spotters and photographers was at Skew Bridge on the WCML, a mile or so south of Preston. On 1 August 1962 a small group of young railway enthusiasts, two partly hidden by the long grass, watch the passing of a Manchester to Workington train that has just run under the bridge which carried the local road to Lostock Hall and Leyland. Unique to British Railways for their Co-Bo wheel arrangement, the twenty Class 28s were built by Metropolitan Vickers in 1958 and fitted with Crossley V8 two-stroke engines that proved problematic from the very beginning. Frequent failures of the noisy and smoky power units saw them returned to the manufacturer in 1961. After a spell on mainly passenger turns, based at Barrow-in-Furness, all members of the class were taken out of service by 1968, just ten or so years after being introduced. The infamous locos though are probably best remembered for their early double-headed runs on the new London to Glasgow *Condor* express freight service, which were immortalised in Terence Cuneo's oil on canvas painting *Night Freight*. (Peter Fitton)

Patricroft 2-6-4T No. 42442 is working hard as it banks the 11.30 train to Newcastle out of Manchester Exchange on 18 August 1962. Of interest in the magnificent station are the three large posters on the wall to the right, highlighted by the morning sun. The first one is advertising Moss Bros the menswear shops, while the middle one, although a little vague, has some connection with Ireland. The final poster, ironically, appears to depict a Sulzer Type 2 on an 'Express Goods', quite possibly the *Condor* train just mentioned. These locos, later known as Class 24s, took over the service when the Co-Bos were unavailable and also took charge of an additional express freight that started in 1963 from Birmingham to Glasgow. (John S. Whiteley)

On the same morning as the previous picture, Hughes Crab No. 42758 passes through Manchester Exchange Station with the 11.45 Manchester Victoria to Southport train. Introduced from 1926, the 2-6-0s numbered 245 in total, being built at both Crewe and Horwich Works. Pictured over to the left is BR Standard No. 73132. (John S. Whiteley)

In this attractive historic scene on 23 March 1963, Stanier 2-6-4 tank No. 42598 has just arrived at Stockport Tiviot Dale station with a stopping train from Liverpool Central. This was a busy freight line, but passenger trains carried few travellers, and closure was not far off. There had once been a loco shed in the yard sidings to the right. Nothing now remains of the railway here as the M60 motorway runs through the site. (Peter Fitton)

The only passenger trains to run on the Preston to Longridge branch after 1930 were specials. The 22 September 1962 was one such day when Super D No. 49451 worked the RCTS *Mid-Lancs Railtour*, which started from Preston's Fishergate Hill station. It is seen here at Grimsargh; the loco ran round at Longridge before heading back to Preston where Horwich Crab No. 42844 took over. This may have been the last sighting of an ex-LNWR engine in use in the area. (Peter Fitton)

At Wyre Dock on 11 May 1963, BR Standard Class 2 No. 84016 stands at the station as passengers are seen alighting from the 1.40 pm Manchester Victoria to Fleetwood service. The 2-6-2T loco, built in October 1953, was in fact allocated for a time to Fleetwood shed during its twelve years working on the main line. (Chris Spring)

The market town of Barnoldswick is in the Borough of Pendle in Lancashire, although prior to 1974 it was part of the historic West Riding of Yorkshire. The station was at the end of a short two-and-a-half-mile branch line that ran off the Colne to Skipton railway, this being closed in February 1970. The once frequent service on the line to Earby, with through workings to Skipton, had already been reduced to a couple of workings for school traffic. On 22 June 1963 though, an enhanced shuttle service was operated for Skipton Gala, and here we see an afternoon arrival behind No. 84015. (Richard Greenwood)

The *Ribble Lune* railtour started off from the Preston East Lancs platform with an afternoon departure time of 13.15. After taking in a section of the soon to be closed Southport line, the train would return to the outskirts of Preston before heading off for Hellifield and Heysham. Ivatt Class 2 No. 46441 was the loco used in the Morecambe area, but the star of the tour was Standard 6P5F 4-6-2 No. 72007 *Clan Mackintosh* seen here at Lancaster Green Ayre on 23 May 1964. The former Midland Railway station would close in January 1966 along with the line via Caton to Wennington. (Gavin Morrison)

A filthy 5X Jubilee No. 45583 *Assam* leaves Blackpool Central with the 2.40pm return weekend extra to Leeds and Bradford on Sunday 20 September 1964, shortly before the station closed. Low Moor engine No. 45565 *Victoria* usually worked this train. (Peter Fitton)

Standard Class 4 No. 75050 was working the 3.02 pm Preston to Liverpool Exchange train on 20 September 1965 when it was photographed here at Lostock Hall Junction after coming round from Todd Lane Junction. The tall signal box, that allowed the bobby to see over the bridge, shows that the Lancashire & Yorkshire once ran the railway here. The line from Preston, that the train had run along, was closed a few years later, along with the signal box, but the other tracks westwards are still busy. (Peter Fitton)

With the town in the background, this was the scene at Horwich station on 20 September 1965 shortly before closure. The loco crew chat as Stanier 2-6-4T No. 42484 waits to take the 4.54 pm workers' train to Bolton; alongside is Standard 2MT 2-6-2 tank No. 84025 which will quickly shunt into the platform when this has departed and leave for Chorley at 4.57 pm. Normally, both trains would be together in the platform. (Peter Fitton)

Looking towards Holme Tunnel in the mid-1960s, a westbound special, probably for Blackpool, reaches the 749-foot summit at Copy Pit complete with signal box, crossover, signals and a row of splendid telegraph poles. The former L&Y railway line from Todmorden to Gannow Junction near Rose Grove saw a regular passenger service of eight trains per weekday and a Saturdays Only through working from Southport Chapel Street right up to its withdrawal on 1 November 1965. A few summertime trains and excursions continued, and although there was a good amount of rail freight, as this dwindled or was diverted away, the mostly 1 in 70 route was pencilled in for closure in 1983. Fortunately, the nine-and-a-half-mile line survived this threat and continues today with two trains an hour each way, one travelling by way of the reopened 400m Todmorden Curve. (Gerry Dixon)

Morecambe Promenade Station was opened by the Midland Railway in 1907 as the terminus for the 'Little North Western' route from Skipton. Part of the route to Lancaster was electrified around 1908 along with the branch line to Heysham, being operated by newly built three-car open sets. On 9 October 1965, Driving Trailer Open Second No. M29021M waits for departure time on a working to Lancaster Castle. The station was closed in February 1994 and replaced by a smaller one situated closer to the town centre. (Gavin Morrison)

A slightly eerie scene at a deserted Liverpool Exchange on 4 January 1966. Preparing to leave on a local service is Stanier 5MT loco No. 45415; built by Armstrong Whitworth and running for exactly thirty years, it was retired from 26C Bolton shed on 31 October 1967. Situated in the centre of the city, Exchange Station was built by the Lancashire and Yorkshire Railway and opened in May 1850 as Tithebarn Street. Badly damaged during the Second World War, it was never fully repaired, and after losing its main services to Liverpool Lime Street during the 1960s it was closed in April 1977. (G. Dixon)

Friday 15 April 1966 being the final day Southport to London trains ran, cleaned-up local Class 5 No. 45156 *Ayrshire Yeomanry* did the honours by working the 15.08 service to Liverpool where it was joined up with a Euston train. Carrying express headlights but with only two carriages and almost as few passengers, the train awaits departure from Southport alongside a 502 unit. By this time the loco's nameplate had been removed and a replacement painted on the backplate; the smokebox number was in the attractive style from the engine's days in Scotland. (Peter Fitton)

Organised by the Epsom Railway Society, *The Mercian* rail tour ran from London Euston to Keighley on 16 April 1967. The route taken included Bescot, Manchester Victoria and Blackburn, from where it took the East Lancs line through to Skipton and finally on to Keighley. A variety of engines was used throughout the journey, starting out with No. E3103 running north to Stockport, followed by No. 45377 and then No. 4472 *Flying Scotsman* returning the special south. The star of the show for many was Gresley K4 loco No. 3442 *The Great Marquess,* seen here trying to make up lost time as it approaches Rishton near Blackburn. Built at Darlington Works in 1938, the 2-6-0 carried the BR No. 61994 on the main line until it was withdrawn in December 1961. Presently, No. 3442 is on static display at the Museum of Scottish Railways at Bo'ness. (John S. Whiteley)

This grand panoramic view of Diggle on 8 July 1967 shows a green liveried Class 40 on an eastbound excursion passing a long mixed freight service that is being held in the goods loop. Built by the London and North Western Railway, the line is about to enter the 3-mile Standedge Tunnel, and although the signal box still remains, the numerous tracks and sidings have long since been removed. Diggle, once located in the West Riding of Yorkshire, had its own station built by the LNWR and opened on 1 August 1849. Efforts by local people to have it reopened have so far proved unsuccessful, meaning the village, now in Greater Manchester, has been without a station since October 1968. (G. Dixon)

Staying on the former LNWR Manchester to Leeds railway, situated at Uppermill is the 23 arch stone Saddleworth Viaduct built in 1849. Here the viaduct crosses the 20-mile long Huddersfield Narrow Canal which was completed in 1811, around 17 years after construction had started. On 22 July 1967, BR Standard Class 5 No. 73053 is in charge of the eastbound 09.30 SO Manchester Exchange to Newcastle service. These 4-6-0 engines were introduced from 1951 with this particular one being built at Derby in June 1954 and continuing running until March 1968. (G. Dixon)

On Boxing Day 1967, a very special train left Carlisle station at 09.45, the last steam hauled passenger train over Shap. The train in question was a football supporters' special to Blackpool. Prior to departure on this glorious clear morning, Britannia Pacific No. 70013 *Oliver Cromwell* had been specially prepared at Kingmoor depot for its memorable trip south. After arrival at Preston the train reversed and, in this view looking south, the Class 7P6F loco makes an impressive picture as it heads towards Fylde Junction and Blackpool. The 4-6-2 was overhauled for BR at Crewe in January 1967 and went on to haul numerous specials before the official end of steam in August 1968. (Paul Riley)

A bird's eye view of the East Lancs side of Preston station from the Vicar's Bridge circa 1968. The bridge spanned the former L&Y route to Bamber Bridge and Blackburn, also giving access to the one-time Joint LNWR/L&Y Park Hotel. In this picture we have the main station in the background, goods warehouses to the right and a local dmu sitting in the EL platforms awaiting departure. Two Class 40s take centre stage, one departing on a passenger service, as the other waits on what appears to be a train of parcel vans. (Stephen Holt)

Another view of the Fleetwood branch, this time on 22 March 1969, just over a year before closure on 1 June 1970. At Thornton-Cleveleys station, a BRCW dmu passes Thornton Station signal box with the 4.06 pm Fleetwood to Poulton-le-Fylde working. An active campaign to re-open the line resulted in a recent feasibility study being undertaken some twenty years after the last freight train used the line. (Chris Spring)

Running down from Moss Lane Junction towards Farington Curve Junction on 29 April 1970 is 1Co-Co1 diesel No. D314 and the 09.00 Liverpool Exchange to Glasgow service. On reaching Preston, additional coaches from Manchester Victoria would be added, a practise that continued into the mid-1980s. This section of railway survives today as a single line through to Ormskirk where passengers must change for Merseyrail trains to Liverpool Central and beyond. (Peter Fitton)

Making its way north along the WCML at Brock on 7 May 1974 is the Royal Train made up of a variety of nine different coaches. Looking resplendent in the morning sunshine are a pair of English Electric Type 4 locos, obviously having paid a recent visit to the paint shop for a coat or two of BR corporate blue. At the head of the train is No. 40027 (formerly named *Parthia*) along with class mate No. 40118 which is presently undergoing overhaul at the Battlefield Line Railway. On entering traffic, they were numbered D227 and D318 respectively. (Peter Fitton)

In May 1980, the 'Rocket 150' celebrations were held to mark the 150th anniversary of the opening of the Manchester to Liverpool Railway and the Rainhill Trials held the previous year. The locomotives for the *Grand Cavalcade* were assembled at Bold Colliery near St. Helens and included many famous steam engines like *Lion*, Nos. 4472 *Flying Scotsman*, 4498 *Sir Nigel Gresley* and 92220 *Evening Star*. In this view at Bold, over to the left the steam locos are being prepared, while adding some brightness to the smoky overcast scene are APT No. 370004 and Deltic No. 55015 *Tulyar*. (John Matthews)

Aintree on Grand National Day 1977 produced half a dozen long distance special trains which reached Sefton Arms station via Edge Hill and the L&Y route from Bootle Junction. After arrival, the empty stock was taken to Edge Hill for servicing, before returning in the late afternoon. Brush Class 47s worked most trains, with Class 40s taking the empty coaches. Here, No. 40132 is pictured passing the former Container Base at Aintree with the 18.25 return working to Glasgow. (Peter Fitton)

A number of special workings ran to bring enthusiasts to the 'Rocket 150' event at Rainhill. On 26 May 1980, an excursion train from London Euston arrives as the spectators start to gather to watch the run past of over 40 steam and diesel locos on each of the three days. At the head of the train is Brush No. 47236, with electric No. 86242 taking a breather as the special nears the end of its 200-mile journey. (Martin Hilbert)

To mark the demise of all BR trains on the Bury to Rawtenstall line the *Rossendale Farewell* rail tour ran on 14 February 1981. Passenger services had ceased from 3 June 1972 with the final coal working to Rawtenstall in December 1980. The six-car dmu left Manchester Victoria at 11.09 before travelling via Castleton and Bury to arrive at Rawtenstall at 14.07, including a sixty-minute break at Bury's Bolton Street station. Seen on the outward journey, the special is crossing the River Irwell near Ramsbottom. After formal closure of the line in 1982, it was re-opened by the East Lancashire Railway Trust in July 1987 with services from Bury to Ramsbottom before extending north to Rawtenstall. (John Matthews)

In the dark and distant past before the appearance of computers, mobile phones and the coming of the digital age, getting hold of details for special trains could be difficult. One particular occasion comes to mind back in the early 1980s, when a small advert in the *Railway Magazine* said that a rail tour was to run from London Euston to Carlisle on 7 March 1981. No further information was forthcoming other than it was titled the *Settle-Carlisle Express* and would be routed via Blackburn and Hellifield after leaving the WCML south of Preston. A telephone call to Blackburn station proved fruitless, and so on the day in question I decided to take a chance and rolled up at a very wet Wilpshire about 10.00. I had only been in place a matter of seconds when through the teeming rain appeared the special with steam aplenty and headed by No. 40080. Although the weather was particularly nasty, things turned out well in the end. (John Matthews)

Recalling the occasion when he took this classic photograph, Les remembers not just that it was very cold, but also the wonderful lighting conditions, ideal for this location near the summit of the climb from Stalybridge. In addition to the picture, two other things came to mind, one was the great sound that disturbed the beautiful wintry stillness, and the other, was the fact that it was now forty years since this never to be forgotten event happened. Nearing Diggle Junction on 17 December 1981 is Deltic No. 55022 *Royal Scots Grey* with the 13.15 Liverpool Lime Street to York train. (Les Nixon)

Well into the1980s, Bolton was a great place to watch trains. Loco-hauled Inter-City and local services could be seen, along with a good variety of freight workings that passed through an almost timeless scene consisting of three signal boxes, a fine array of semaphore signals and both goods and parcels depots. With Holy Trinity Church as a backdrop, No. 47338 runs past Bolton West box and on to the Blackburn line with the *Cumberland Sausage* special from Manchester Victoria to Sellafield. (John Matthews)

Departing Preston and crossing the NU Bridge over the River Ribble is diesel No. 25221 with the 19.14 Blackpool North to Manchester Victoria train on 20 June 1983. The North Union Railway came about with the amalgamation of the Wigan Branch and the Preston and Wigan Railways in May 1834 and continued until it was absorbed jointly by the LNWR and L&Y companies in July 1889. Built at Derby, No. D7571 was new to Cricklewood in October 1963 and after receiving its later number in February 1974, it continued working for a further ten years before withdrawal on 31 January 1984. (John Matthews)

An early start on the morning of 29 October 1983 for 'Peak' No. 45120 with a westbound mystery excursion from Nelson. Along with *Merrymaker* and *Rail Rambler* specials, 'Mystexes' as they were known, were very popular trains of the time, taking passengers to many out of the way locations. The earlier empty coaching stock would have reversed in Chaffers Sidings, just to the west of Colne, before the train set off for its secret destination, picking up at Burnley where it is seen crossing the attractive viaduct. The through route from Colne to Skipton was closed in February 1970, but the Skipton-East Lancashire Rail Action Partnership (SELRAP) are very active in striving to reinstate the 11.5 miles of railway. (John Matthews)

Two Class 503 Wirral and Mersey Three-Car Sets run past Bidston East Junction with a train for Liverpool on 21 January 1984. The connection to the Docks diverges to the left in the distance. The attractive looking signal box located in a great industrial landscape was closed in September 1994. (Paul Shannon)

To commemorate 150 years of brewing beer, Wilsons Brewery of Newton Heath ran a number of Anniversary Specials on 11 July 1984. At the grand looking Manchester Victoria station LNWR coal tank No. 1054 is pictured with one of the special trains. The 0-6-2T loco was built at Crewe in 1888 and carried No. 58926 while under British Railways from 1948; it is now owned by the National Trust. (John Cooper Smith)

The *Mayflower & Galatea* special was run by Hertfordshire Railtours on 15 December 1984. Right from the beginning things didn't run too smoothly, with a 60-minute delayed start from London Marylebone. By the time 'Peak' No. 45141 and the train had reached Bare Lane this had only been reduced by three minutes as the train headed for Heysham and later to Barrow-in-Furness.
(John Matthews)

On 20 April 1985, the Birmingham Branch of the engine drivers' union ASLEF organised a special charter from Redditch to Carlisle, pictured approaching Gisburn. Against the background of many UK railway companies increasing the working week from 60 to 66 hours, reducing wages and making the 12-hour working day commonplace, the Associated Society of Locomotive Engineers and Firemen was formed in 1880. At the head of the special train, photographed as it climbs away from Pendle Hill, is loco No. 47609. It was built at Crewe in 1965 and first ran as D1656, but later carried the name *Prince William* when numbered 47798. (John Matthews)

Just a few weeks before the mass withdrawal of the remaining Class 40 locos, the RESL *Royal Scot* special took to the rails on 28 December 1984. After the end of January 1985, only No. 40122 (D200) was still in operation, being seen on various rail tours and Settle to Carlisle workings until 1988. Just north of Preston at a grey and misty Brock, Nos. 40152 and 40086 are seen powering the train to Glasgow Central, from where No. 26042 would take over for a short trip to Polmadie. (John Matthews)

A return to Copy Pit on the morning of 1 June 1985 sees EE Type 3 No. 37215 reaching the summit with the Saturdays Only Sheffield to Blackpool North train. Often hauled by a Class 37 locomotive and running over this particular line, it was a very popular working for the enthusiasts of the day and the odd holidaymaker. New to traffic in January 1964, the loco was allocated to Landore and spent over three years in South Wales before moving north to Healey Mills in October 1967. At present, No. 37215 can be seen in preservation at the Gloucestershire Warwickshire Railway. (John Matthews)

Approaching Miles Platting from the east is Brush loco No. 47455 with the 09.55 Scarborough-Liverpool Lime Street Trans-Pennine service. Photographed from Miles Platting station on 25 January 1986, things are very different today, with the station having been closed in 1995 and electrification of the line from Manchester Victoria to Stalybridge now in full swing. (John Matthews)

When this photograph was taken on 16 April 1986 the power station at Stalybridge had been closed for over six years but was not demolished until 1989. With a Liverpool Lime Street to Newcastle train in tow Class 47 No. 47421 heads east along the former LNWR line towards Diggle. The Brush engine, built in 1963, originally carried No. D1520 before being re-numbered in January 1974; it was named *Brontes of Haworth* at the KWVR in August 1985. (Peter Fitton)

In the days when a large number of West Coast Main Line trains were diverted via Blackburn and the Settle to Carlisle line, these didn't just run in the daytime. In addition, virtually a full timetable of overnight and sleeper trains could also be seen, if you were keen or mad enough to spend the night on Blackburn station. Southbound, two Glasgow to London Euston trains, a Glasgow to Plymouth, an Edinburgh to Euston, plus the Stranraer-Euston and Inverness Sleeper services all passed through. Viewed here in the early hours of 4 April 1988 is No. 47645 with the 17.42 Fort William to Euston Sleeper. (John Matthews)

By the time of this picture on 17 September 1988 Carnforth East signal box was very rarely in use except for the odd special working. On this very wet and dismal morning there were in fact two special trains that ran through from F&M Junction and therefore avoided Carnforth station. Both ran from Barrow-in-Furness to York; the first was hauled by Crewe based No. 47427, while the second, pictured here, had No. 47657 at the front. In late 1989 the section of railway between F&M and East junctions was taken out of use. (John Matthews)

With dmus in short supply at the time, Class 31 No. 31467 was pressed into service with a four-coach train consisting of three Network SouthEast Mk1s. On 6 July 1990, the 09.40 Manchester Victoria to Oldham and Blackpool North train can be seen near Shaw. A total of 263 of the class were built by Brush Traction between 1957 and 1962, and by 1974 they were allocated mainly to the Eastern Region and four London sheds: Finsbury Park (51), Old Oak Common (19), Stratford (24) and Cricklewood (2). (Paul Shannon)

On 25 May 1992, the Football League Second Division Play-off Final took place at Wembley Stadium between Blackburn Rovers and Leicester City. A couple of special football excursions ran to take supporters from the East Lancashire town to King's Cross, and nearing Holme, on the climb towards Copy Pit, is No. 47575 with the first of these. Appearing on the main line in October 1964 with two-tone green livery and numbered D1770, the engine by this time was now looking bright and shiny in its Res (Parcels Sector) colours. (John Matthews)

Sunday 26 April 1992 saw Pathfinder Tours run a series of short rail trips called the *Lancastrian Mini Excursions*. Identified as 'Train 2' on the day was the 11.12 Manchester Victoria to Blackburn and the 12.22 return which was routed via Darwen and Bolton. On the outward journey Nos. 37891 and 37298 provided the motive power, while the return trip was handled by No. 56091 *Castle Donnington Power Station*, photographed departing Blackburn. Further trips to Southport and Morecambe ran during the day with the assistance of double-headed Class 20 and 31 locomotives. (John Matthews)

Starting off from Swindon behind No. 47823, Pathfinders Tours' the *Two Roses Voyager* crosses Entwistle Viaduct on the Blackburn to Bolton West Pennine Line. With a train of ten coaches behind, EE Type 1 locos Nos. 20121 and 20214 are returning from their visit to Scarborough and will pass through a number of red and white rose locations including Leeds, Hebden Bridge, Manchester, Stockport and Sheffield. The picture was taken at 18.20 on the 19 July 1992. (Peter Fitton)

At a deserted Blackpool North Station on 12 June 1992 is No. 37278 waiting to leave with the 07.06 to Manchester Victoria. Not a common visitor to the Fylde, the loco would more usually be found on coal workings which is shown by its smart BR Railfreight Coal Sector livery. An extremely popular class of loco with trainmen and enthusiasts alike, and by 2020 there were still around seventy registered for main line working. (Peter Fitton)

Whalley station had been closed for over thirty years when this photograph was taken on the 24 April 1993. Class 60 loco No. 60094 had earlier worked south as far as Preston with a late running Edinburgh to Birmingham train and here we see it returning north with No. 47973 on the diverted 10.15 Euston-Glasgow service. Whalley was reopened for passenger trains in May 1994 after extensive renovation work to this and other stations on the Ribble Valley Line. (John Matthews)

The station at Midge Hall near Preston was opened by the Lancashire and Yorkshire Railway in October 1859, around ten years after the opening of the line, first proposed by the Liverpool, Ormskirk and Preston Railway in 1846. The original LYR signal box was replaced by the more modern structure in 1972, and still controls the road crossing today, as well as the only surviving semaphore signal for many a mile. Usually consigned to the hourly passing of diesel units, Midge Hall witnessed something a little different on 22 May 1993, when this special train from Crewe to Heysham visited the line. The leading engine No. 56027 is out of view at the head of the train as it continues along the single line to Rufford with No. 37706 bringing up the rear. (John Matthews)

Another ex-LYR route that survives today is the one that makes its way along the Ribble Valley linking Blackburn and Hellifield. This 23.45-mile railway, starting off in Lancashire, runs north-east via Clitheroe before joining up with the former Midland Railway line in North Yorkshire. In the days before the ill-conceived idea of running rail replacement bus services, the route saw a great number of diverted trains when the WCML was closed north of Preston. On 18 November 1995, No. 47716 crosses the eight-arch stone built Stockbeck Viaduct after emerging from Gisburn Tunnel with the 08.30 Euston to Glasgow Central service. (John Matthews)

Unfortunately, a 30-minute delay wasn't the best start for the *White Horse Rambler*, seen here a little before leaving Preston on 22 January 2000. At the front of the rail tour is Bo-Bo No. 33103 that would take the train to Appleford Sidings near Didcot and include a visit to the Highworth Branch and an impressive climb up the 1 in 37 Lickey Bank. The Class 33 locos were built between 1960 and 1962 by the Birmingham Railway and Carriage Company and were a more powerful development of the Type 2 Class 26s. Out of the ninety-eight produced, nineteen were modified for push-pull operation on the Southern Region; these becoming Class 33/1s not Class 34s as originally planned. At present, No. 33103 is preserved at the nine-mile Ecclesbourne Valley Railway in Derbyshire, which has operated train services along the former Midland Railway Wirksworth Branch since October 2002. (John Matthews)

During the winter months the sun doesn't reach many parts of the Cliviger Gorge, including the climb towards Copy Pit summit. Luckily, Saturday 28 December 2005 was a fair-weather day and with the help of a sprinkling of snow, the landscape was pretty bright for the passing of the *Fusilier Farewell* special. Organised by the Deltic Preservation Society, it was run to say goodbye to No. 55019 *Royal Highland Fusilier* before its withdrawal from main line operations. Starting from Derby, the tour was routed via Chesterfield and Sheffield before arriving at York, where a break was taken while the engine ran round. From York the 13-coach train ran to Leeds, next heading off down the Calder Valley and turning right at Hall Royd Junction for Rose Grove and the East Lancs line to Blackburn. The return to York and Derby saw the train pass through Manchester Victoria and take the route over Diggle and Huddersfield. (John Matthews)

Mossley station is the location for this great shot of the *Cotton Mill Express* that ran from Manchester Victoria to Blackburn on 27 September 2008. The driver had slowed Jubilee No. 5690 to 5mph through the platform, a tricky task, but the train actually stopped and here we see the loco re-starting on the uphill gradient. (Peter Fitton)

Another Deltic, this time No. 55022 *Royal Scots Grey*, crossing Strand Road, Preston with the *Ribble-Lune* rail tour of 10 October 2010. In some ways, the spiritual home of the Class 55 locomotive, as the prototype DP1 *Deltic* was built at the Dick, Kerr & Co. works based on Strand Road. The Branch Line Society special had run up from Crewe, but delays in the Northwich area meant a 60-minute late arrival at the Ribble Steam Railway museum. Some time was recovered on the next part of the journey north, but on reaching Morecambe and Heysham Power Station it was still over 30 minutes behind time. The eight-coach train was top and tailed throughout, with No. 66066 taking a good share of the work. (John Matthews)

When the barriers go down at Bamber Bridge level crossing virtually everything stops, especially the road traffic, that soon backs up as far as the eye can see. Station Road, formerly part of the A6, is the main village thoroughfare located three miles south-east of Preston. Usually, only dmus to Colne and York plus the odd freight train require the assistance of the distinctive looking signal box, but with all signalling controlled from Preston Power Box it now only controls the crossing and two others further down the line to Blackburn. Concerns over the stability of the box led to the Meccano ironwork being erected a few years ago; this is clearly visible as Black Five locos Nos. 44871 and 45407 head east with a Manchester Victoria to Carlisle steam special on 13 April 2019. (John Matthews)

WEST YORKSHIRE

Prior to 1974 the county was known as the West Riding of Yorkshire and today is made up of the five boroughs of Bradford, Calderdale, Kirklees, City of Leeds and the City of Wakefield. The industrial landscape of West Yorkshire was very much tied up in the manufacture of wool, cloth and mining of coal. Strange as it may seem, rhubarb is still grown today in large quantities in what is called the 'Rhubarb Triangle'. The county is also a major financial centre with many well-known banks and building societies based there. The railways arrived in the 1830s and soon four railway companies, the Great Northern, L&YR, LNWR and Midland, were all busy building lines to all parts of the county.

Moving on to West Yorkshire, the first image is at Lightcliffe station which was opened by the LYR in 1850 and is situated three miles east of Halifax. On 5 May 1959, Ivatt 2-6-2T No. 41250 arrives with the Bradford portion of a Leeds Central to Liverpool Exchange service. Calder Valley trains continued to call at the village station until closure came on 14 June 1965. (Gavin Morrison)

Viewed from the footbridge that crossed over the line near Copley Hill shed is the southbound *Yorkshire Pullman*. On 28 May 1960, local Class A1 loco No. 60134 *Foxhunter* heads the express for King's Cross. Starting out in 1923 as the *Harrogate Pullman Limited*, the train soon changed its name to the *West Riding Pullman* and ran through to Newcastle. In 1935, it returned to Harrogate again with a through portion for Hull detached at Doncaster. (Gavin Morrison)

Arriving at Hall Royd Junction after running down from Copy Pit is a Blackpool to Chesterfield Saturday Only service pictured on 6 August 1960. To the left can be seen the sidings located in the triangle of lines running from Todmorden to Burnley and Hebden Bridge, while at the head of the train is Class 9F No. 92059. Locomotive shed masters in 1959/60 were finding these locos provided ideal power for such trains. However, higher BR authority became concerned as reports of high speeds into the nineties were being recorded and prohibited their use. The 2-10-0 loco was built in 1955 and after spending some time at Warrington Dallam shed, it was withdrawn from Birkenhead in September 1966. (Richard Greenwood)

Ready to leave Leeds Central with the 12.30 to King's Cross on 16 May 1961 is Gresley A3 No. 60108 *Gay Crusader*. Named after the racehorse that completed the 1917 Triple Crown, the loco was in service for 40 years, being withdrawn from 36A Doncaster shed in November 1963. (Gavin Morrison)

Leeds Holbeck allocated Britannia Class 7P6F No. 70044 *Earl Haig* leaves Leeds City with the Down *Waverley* on 8 March 1961. Built at Crewe in 1953, the 4-6-2 had a short lifespan completing only thirteen years on the main line before the end came at Stockport Edgeley in October 1966. (Gavin Morrison)

Holbeck 55A was the main shed at Leeds, having a large and varied allocation of engines for both local and longer distance passenger workings. On 17 April 1961, Royal Scot Class No. 46117 *Welsh Guardsman* awaits its next working along with Nos. 73171, 92050, 92157 and 45605 *Cyprus*. (John S. Whiteley)

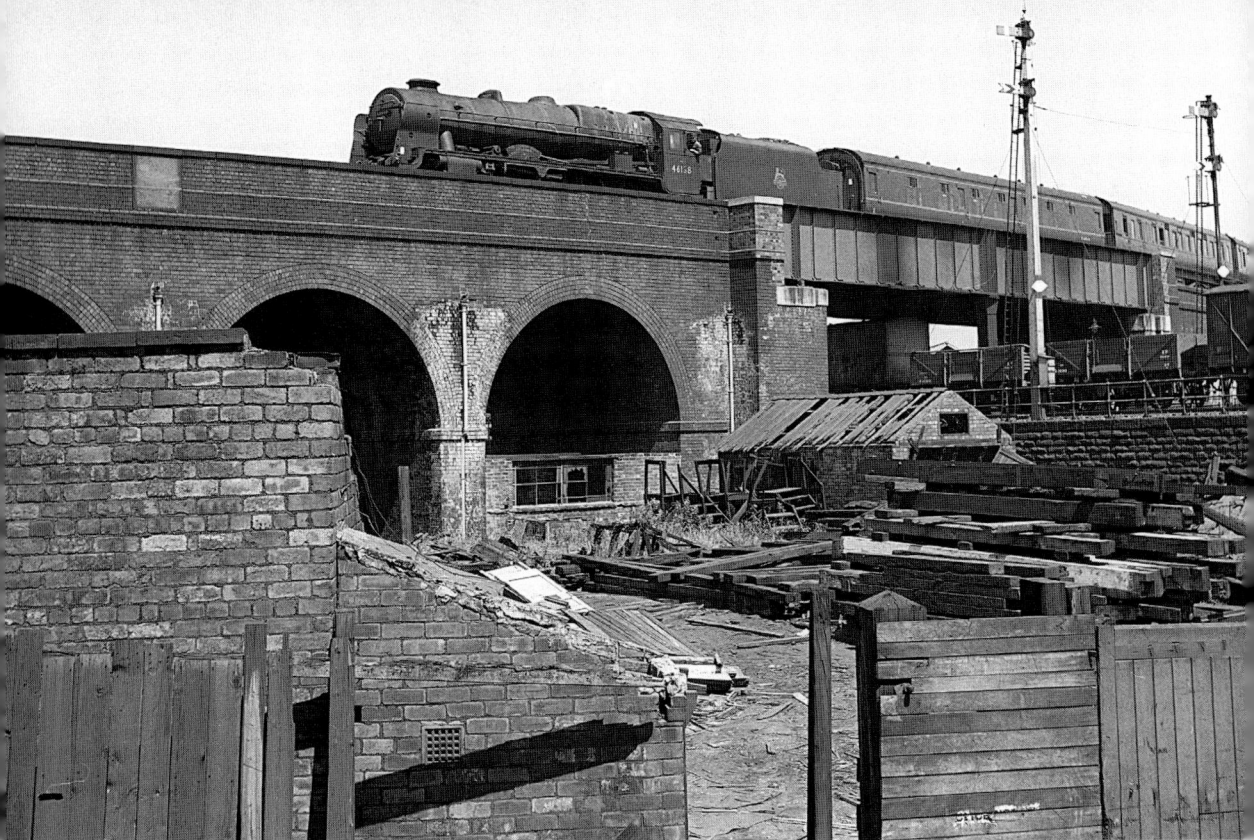

The 12.38 Leeds City to Manchester Exchange was a Summer Only working, seen crossing the viaduct over Leeds Holbeck shed on 29 June 1961. At the front of the train is rebuilt Scot No. 46138 *The London Irish Rifleman*; built by the North British Locomotive Company, Glasgow in 1927, it originally carried LMS number 6138. (Gavin Morrison)

An extremely atmospheric image here as B1 No. 61320 appears out of the smoke and fog at Copley Hill and is caught by the low winter sunlight. Climbing away from Leeds, this is the Bradford portion of the Sunday *Harrogate Pullman* on 28 January 1962. (John S. Whiteley)

Approaching Leeds City Station on 31 March 1962 we see Jubilee Class No. 45697 *Achilles* heading the southbound *Devonian*. The train would have started out from Bradford Forster Square. Built at Crewe in 1936, the Stanier 4-6-0 was in service for a further five years before withdrawal from nearby Holbeck in September 1967. (John S. Whiteley)

Creating a more than impressive sight as it struggles away from Leeds Central is Gresley A4 No. 60029 *Woodcock*. The train, pictured on Sunday 1 April 1962, is the heavy 17.00 express to King's Cross. Built at Doncaster for the LNER, the thirty-five streamlined engines started work on the East Coast Main Line in 1935 and some continued right through to 1966 after being transferred to Scotland and seeing out their time on the Aberdeen-Glasgow expresses. (John S. Whiteley)

On the same day, Gresley V2 No. 60907 of York prepares to leave Leeds City station with the 14.45 train to Newcastle. Built in 1940, apart from a few weeks in 1952 when it was reallocated to Darlington, No. 60907 spent its entire life based at York from where it was withdrawn in late May 1962. The train is standing in what was originally called Leeds New, opened jointly by the LNWR and NER in 1869 but was combined with the former Wellington station in 1939 which had been built by the MR and renamed Leeds City. It was rebuilt in 1967 when nearby Central station closed and services transferred to Leeds City and was further rebuilt and refurbished between 1999 and 2002, looking very different than it did in 1962. (John S. Whiteley)

Based at Carnforth shed, Jubilee No. 45686 *St. Vincent* is passing the site of Holbeck Lower station which was closed on 7 July 1958. The Stanier 4-6-0, built at Crewe Works in February 1936, is at the head of the 13.54 Leeds-Carnforth service on 1 May 1962, just six months before being stopped for the last time at its home depot. (Gavin Morrison)

Passing its home shed 'Copley Hill' on 1 July 1962 is the Sundays' 16.40 Leeds City to King's Cross service. Providing the power is Peppercorn designed A1 No. 60117 *Bois Roussel*; built at Doncaster in October 1948, the 4-6-2 loco was one of a class of 49 that had all been withdrawn by June 1966, previous to this No. 60117 was withdrawn a year earlier from Ardsley. (John S. Whiteley)

Although there is not a passenger train in sight, it would have been a shame not to include this great image of times gone by. Wetherby station was built by the North Eastern Railway on the Cross Gates to Wetherby line and was known as Linton Road. Opened in 1902, it replaced an earlier station in York Road dating from May 1876. Passenger services fell to the Beeching axe and were withdrawn in January 1964. In this view, captured on 25 September 1965, is Thompson B1 No. 61224 at Wetherby East. (Gavin Morrison)

You wait ages for a B1 loco to appear then two come along together. This one, No. 61406, is passing Wakefield Westgate on a wintry 23 January 1965 with a Cleethorpes to Leeds working. Built between 1942 and 1952, a total of 410 of these mixed traffic locos were produced, including 136 that were built for British Railways after nationalisation in 1948. The class carried various names; the first forty-one were named after antelopes, some later ones after LNER directors. This gave rise to the long and short of locomotive naming; No. 61221 *Sir Alexander Erskine-Hill* one of the longest and No. 61018 *Gnu* the shortest. (Peter Fitton)

On the same day at Wakefield Westgate, Deltic No. D9014 is approaching with an express from Leeds, while another B1, No. 61189 *Sir William Gray,* waits with some coaches from Bradford, which will be attached to the Leeds train and then continue to King's Cross. Running in BR green livery and named *The Duke of Wellington's Regiment,* the diesel was later numbered 55014 and carried on working along the East Coast Main Line until November 1981. (Peter Fitton)

Steam locos were still being used to work some trains on the former Midland Railway route from Leeds City to Bradford Forster Square in 1965, most being portions of long-distance expresses. On 1 April, Manningham shed's Fairburn tank No. 42189 is seen arriving at Shipley with three coaches from Birmingham New Street, as a Britannia heads for Leeds in the distance. (Peter Fitton)

Preparing to leave Leeds City for Morecambe Promenade on 17 August 1965 is former LMS Stanier Black 5 No. 45328. Trains still connect West Yorkshire with the seaside town of Morecambe and in 2022 there were eight services through to Morecambe via Lancaster, the first two starting out from Skipton and Bradford Forster Square. Worth noting is that the 10.18 Leeds departure has a connection to Heysham Port for the sailing to the Isle of Man. The 1965 timetable showed a similar frequency of trains but the final one, the 21.32 from Leeds, while also running to Heysham, at this time connected with the sea crossing to Belfast departing at 23.55. (John Cooper Smith)

An atmospheric picture of Bradford Forster Square station on 24 November 1965. One of the footplate crew looks back to check all is in order as he waits for departure time on the 15.40 to Carlisle. Pacific 4-6-2 No. 72006 *Clan Mackenzie* is providing the motive power for the long run over the Settle to Carlisle line, that would take over three and a half hours and make calls at twenty stations along the way. One of ten Clan class engines built at Crewe in early 1952, No. 72006 was withdrawn from Kingmoor in May 1966. A proposal for a further build of fifteen locos was scheduled but after a number of delays this was scrapped. (Peter Fitton)

A quick look back at Leeds sees BR Standard Class 4 No. 75057 waiting to return to its home shed with a local working to Skipton. Creating plenty of smoke and steam, the Swindon built engine has only a few weeks left in service before withdrawal in late February 1966. Platform 6 appears to have plenty of parcels and sundry goods waiting to be loaded before departure on 8 January 1966. (John Cooper Smith)

Heading up Cliviger Gorge and crossing the county boundary between Lancashire and West Yorkshire is Jubilee No. 45565 *Victoria* with a working to Blackpool on 28 May 1966. The engine is pulling hard as it passes through Portsmouth on the climb to the summit at Copy Pit. Sitting high above the fourth carriage from the end of the train, the distinctive signal box was kept busy controlling the level crossing, signals and points, now mostly a distant memory. (Gerald Dixon)

Approaching Mirfield on 6 August 1966 is No. 45565 *Victoria* again with the 13.25 Saturday Only train from Blackpool North to Leeds. The location is Heaton Lodge Junction where the lines from the Calder Valley (L&Y) and Huddersfield (LNWR) meet. Already over thirty years old, the Jubilee Class loco ran for another five months before being retired at Low Moor in January 1967. (G. Dixon)

On the 1 in 50 climb out of Bradford Exchange, the last Fowler 2-6-4T No. 42410 powers the 09.15 Blackpool service towards Halifax. Here, the five coaches would be attached to the main train from Leeds City, this being hauled by a Jubilee Class engine for its journey over the Pennines. (Peter Fitton)

Wakefield B1 No. 61030 *Nyala* leaves Bradford Exchange with the 15.05 to King's Cross on a sunny 10 September 1966. The train would run to Wakefield to be attached to the main train from Leeds and be diesel hauled onwards. This view, as the train emerges from beneath Wakefield Road Bridge, would be lost when Interchange station replaced Exchange in the early 1970s. The engine was to be one of the last of its class to be overhauled but didn't remain clean for very long. (Peter Fitton)

Just prior to leaving Leeds City on 14 October 1966 is a Jubilee Class 4-6-0 with the 17.28 special Friday working to Blackpool North. Built by the NBLC in August 1934, the Stanier loco No. 45562 *Alberta* had just over a year to run, being stopped at Holbeck for the final time in November 1967. (Peter Fitton)

On 30 October 1966, Low Moor MPD's Fairburn tank No. 42116 was in charge of the 10.28 Sunday service to King's Cross when this view was taken inside Bradford Exchange Station. The train, seen on the GNR side of the station, would travel to Wakefield to couple to the main portion from Leeds. One year later, all steam had finished here. Interestingly, No. 42116 never received the later BR crest. (Peter Fitton)

Arriving at Leeds Central on 18 April 1967 is Fairburn 4P loco No. 42055 having run over from Bradford with the 08.00 train to King's Cross. The joint station was opened on 18 September 1854, but after 113 years it closed on 1 May 1967, although the last train had departed for Harrogate in the early evening of 29 April. (Peter Fitton)

Unlike today, Bradford Forster Square was a busy place with several platforms and a very large goods yard area. As well as dmus on local trains, there were loco hauled ones to Carlisle, Leeds and Morecambe plus parcels traffic. On 29 April 1967, Peak D121 was photographed leaving with the five coach 09.13 to Leeds which will be attached there to the main train to London St. Pancras. In those days, many spare coaches were to be seen in carriage sidings, some seeing very little use. Today the tracks here are both simplified and electrified with the goods traffic all gone, but there are still trains to London. (Peter Fitton)

Another view of the *Yorkshire Pullman,* this time at Bradford Exchange in the summer of 1967. At the head of the train is Stanier 4-6-0 No. 44693, built at Horwich Works in 1950, while out of sight behind the lead engine is, I am reliably informed, another Black Five loco. (Gavin Morrison)

A great scene looking east at Standedge on 7 July 1967. The photographer was certainly at the right place at the right time, being lucky enough to capture the two trains together. A Peak heads a Trans-Pennine service for Manchester while a grubby looking 9F waits on a long tank train. (G. Dixon)

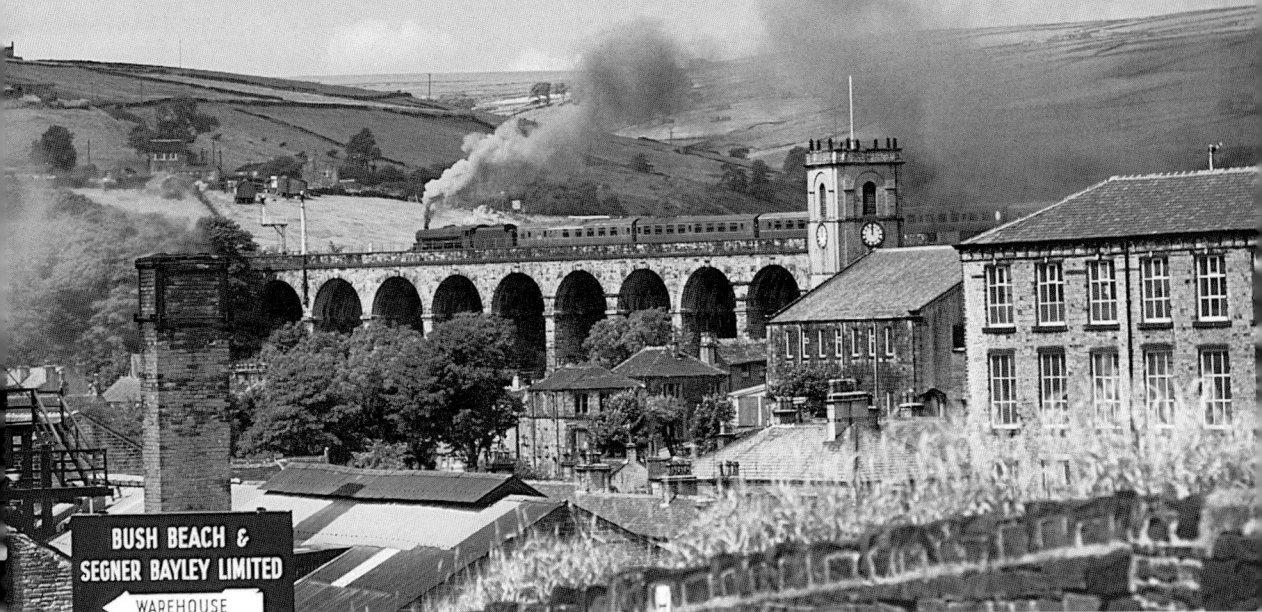

An excellent mixture of both the rural and the industrial are combined in this image of Slaithwaite on 22 July 1967. The village is in the Colne Valley, about five miles south-west of Huddersfield, and lies across the Huddersfield Narrow Canal and the River Colne. Illustrated by the mills in the photograph is the fact that the economy was once heavily dependent on wool and yarns. Crossing the viaduct is the 09.20 SO Scarborough to Manchester train headed by Stanier 4-6-0 No. 45219. (G. Dixon)

On Bradford Exchange Platform 8, green Type 2 loco No. 5147 (25147) is about to depart with the *Devonian* for Plymouth on 10 April 1971. In the distance, another class member also prepares to leave on a King's Cross working from Platform 10. The impressive looking train shed sadly didn't survive too much longer.
(Peter Fitton)

Opened by the L&Y Railway in September 1879, the 3.5-mile Clayton West branch ran east off the Huddersfield to Penistone line between Shepley and Denby Dale. Viewed on 26 May 1981 is a local dmu from Huddersfield, while on the station building to the left is the 'Withdrawal of Passenger Services' notice. After closure of the railway, it was re-opened in 1991 as the Kirklees 15-inch Light Railway, later being rebranded as the Whistlestop Valley line. (John Matthews)

On the morning of 31 October 1981, there was a very early start for the *Citadel Express* to Carlisle, departing Plymouth at 04.00. Later in the day, it is photographed passing through Keighley behind No. 50011 *Centurion*. The same loco headed the special throughout, running up the former Midland Railway to Carlisle before returning south via the West Coast Main Line. (John Matthews)

Approaching Huddersfield on the bright morning of 27 August 1983 is the 07.10 York-Liverpool Lime Street train hauled by Peak No. 45120. At this time numerous loco-hauled services could be seen along this former LNWR route, and as well as the regular Trans-Pennine services, additional holiday trains to Blackpool, North Wales and Scarborough would add to the interest of the day. These appeared behind a variety of locos, including Classes 31, 40, 45, 46 and 47. (John Matthews)

Easter Monday 1982 was a good day for the travelling fans of Sheffield United and an even better one if you had a liking for Class 45 locomotives. On that day, the visiting team soundly beat fellow Division 4 side Halifax Town 5-1, plus their followers also had the pleasure of a journey back to Sheffield on this football special, caught departing Halifax behind Peak No. 45023 *The Royal Pioneer Corps*. (John S. Whiteley)

In the early hours of 10 February 1985, Class 40 loco No. 40122 (D200) waits at Huddersfield with the empty stock from the previous day's *St. Andrew* rail tour. Starting out from Bolton, the train travelled by way of Leeds and York to reach its destination at Edinburgh Waverley. The special's run was far from trouble free with the Type 4 encountering a lack of heating, and although a failed attempt to rectify this was made at Newcastle, the freezing train was forced to continue on through the snow. Also, a circular trip from Dunfermline to Thornton Yard and Kirkcaldy was shelved because of late running. (Peter Fitton)

Located at the confluence of three steep-sided Pennine valleys, Todmorden sits in the Upper Calder Valley part of West Yorkshire. At one time, the Lancashire and Yorkshire boundary ran through the centre of the town, and still today the cricket club is the only Yorkshire team playing in the Lancashire League. High above the Rochdale Canal, the former Manchester to Leeds Railway crosses over Gauxholme No. 2 viaduct featuring its beautiful cast iron arch and castellated abutments. About to pass over the bridge on 8 December 1985 is the 11.56 Manchester Victoria-Leeds train. (John Matthews)

Approaching Huddersfield on 14 November 1987 is the Pathfinder Tours *Skipton Skipper* special from Bristol Temple Meads. The train had travelled up via Birmingham, Toton and Sheffield prior to taking the Penistone to Huddersfield line. Motive power was provided by No. 50020 *Revenge* with a little assistance from No. 31463 during its visit to Ilkley and Bradford Forster Square stations. (Peter Fitton)

Originally booked for haulage by a Class 45/1 loco, the *Border Fellsman* prepares to restart after a 10-minute photo stop at Hebden Bridge. On 15 April 1989, the unavailability of a Peak meant that Nos. 31446 and 31405 took over the train at Birmingham New Street, this having arrived from Swindon behind Brush No. 47648. After running along the Calder Valley, the special train made its way to Skipton and finally Carlisle. (John Matthews)

Compared with the earlier picture taken from a similar spot on the Burnley to Todmorden line at Portsmouth, little appears to remain other than the high hills, sweeping track and the odd house. Almost twenty-four years separate the images, with this later view of a BR Class 141 dmu running down from Copy Pit summit operating the 11.46 Blackpool North to York service on 9 March 1990. Manufactured by British Leyland, No. 141119 was one of 12 Class 141s exported to the Islamic Republic of Iran Railways around 2001. (John Matthews)

The unique Class 89 electric prototype locomotive was built in 1986 at British Rail's Crewe Works. Capable of producing over 6,000bhp, No. 89001 first appeared on the main line in February 1987 and after moving to Bounds Green depot it commenced working on ECML services. Following painting in the new style Inter City Swallow colours, the loco was named *Avocet* at King's Cross station in January 1989. Seen at Leeds in GNER livery, No. 89001 waits for departure with the 11.03 train to King's Cross. (Gavin Morrison)

Seen as a goodbye to the Class 56 locomotive, the *Twilight Grids* rail tour ran on 31 March 2004. Fortunately, things didn't turn out as planned, and around eighteen years later a small number of the class can still be found operating on the main line. The special ran from Bristol to York, and was initially hauled by No. 56115, before No. 56078 took over at York for a trip across the Pennines and back. Surprisingly running 45 minutes early, No. 56078 appears out of Millwood Tunnel and passes through Hall Royd Junction on its way to Manchester where it would take the Diggle line back to York. (John Matthews)

NORTH YORKSHIRE

The county is one of many contrasts, from the thriving tourist spots of York, Harrogate and Scarborough to the vast open areas of farmland. It is not surprising then that the main source of work is in agriculture, along with looking after the Yorkshire Dales and North York Moors National Parks. Certainly, the jewel in the crown of North Yorkshire must be the historic city of York itself, with its Minster dating from 1472. Other popular visitor attractions include the Shambles, National Railway Museum and Jorvick Viking Centre. To see York Station's magnificent curved roof is worth the trip alone, but for those looking to step back in time there are a number of heritage lines, including the North Yorkshire Moors and Wensleydale railways.

Organised by the RCTS, the *Yorkshire Coast Rail Tour* ran from Leeds to Whitby on 23 June 1957. Setting out via York, the train visited Gilling, Bridlington and Scarborough before arriving at Whitby station where a photo-stop was taken. During the stop, locos 69881 and 62731 *Selkirkshire* take a breather prior to returning to Leeds via Pickering. (Gavin Morrison)

Having just run through Skipton station prior to passing under the Grassington Branch is a local Morecambe to Leeds train photographed on 22 August 1959. Based at Skipton for a time, the Ivatt 2-6-0 No. 43113 was built at Horwich in April 1951, and ran for fifteen years before withdrawal from Crewe South in September 1966. Distinguished by their high-level running plates, the Class 4 locos were referred to as Doodlebugs by many railwaymen. One engine was saved from scrapping, No. 43106 now runs in preservation at the Severn Valley Railway. (Gavin Morrison)

Starting off from York on 23 March 1961 is Peppercorn Pacific No. 60158 *Aberdonian* working a northbound express to Newcastle. The 49 Class A1 locos were built at Doncaster and Darlington Works with No. 60158 making its main line debut in November 1949. Designed to work the heaviest trains on the ECML from King's Cross to Edinburgh, by the summer of 1966 all the class had been withdrawn after a late attempt to preserve No. 60145 *Saint Mungo* had failed. (John S. Whiteley)

In this moody image of 31 March 1961, the old and the new stand in front of what is now the National Railway Museum at York. A pair of English Electric Type 4s, Nos. D285 and D275, both only a year or so old, are pictured alongside Jubilee No. 45577 *Bengal* of Bristol Barrow Road and a New England 9F, No. 92143.

(John S. Whiteley)

Approaching Holgate Bridge, York on 16 June 1962 is Class A3 No. 60112 *St. Simon* complete with small smoke deflectors. Heading south for King's Cross, the express runs through Holgate Junction where the station avoiding lines sweep in from the left. The 4-6-2 would continue in service for another two years or so before being withdrawn from New England shed on 26 December 1964. The loco by that date would have completed an impressive forty-one years on the main line. (Gavin Morrison)

In this rare scene, photographed by Ken Roberts, a Peak diesel loco runs south through Ingleton with a diverted *Thames Clyde Express* around 1962. Ingleton was located on the Clapham Junction to Low Gill line and was a meeting place for the Midland Railway from the south and the LNWR arriving from the north. Trains from both companies terminated at the station, and although passenger services ceased in January 1954 goods traffic continued until 1965.

The RCTS *Mid Lancs Railtour*, starting from Preston West Lancs Goods, or Fishergate Hill station as it was known, covered a number of secondary routes across Lancashire and North Yorkshire during its journey on 22 September 1962. At Grassington the special reversed and headed back to Skipton, where the Crab 2-6-0 No. 42844 continued with the five-coach train back along the East Lancs route to Preston. (Peter Fitton)

Running through the open countryside at Otterburn, just south of Hellifield, is Stanier Black Five No. 44877. Heading north on 4 June 1963, the loco, built at Crewe in April 1945, is hauling the 10.47 Leeds to Morecambe stopping service. Withdrawn from Carnforth shed, No. 44877 ran until the end of steam on BR in August 1968. (Peter Fitton)

Another Black Five arrives at Skipton with a seven-coach train from the north. On 27 September 1963, No. 45306 is blowing off steam as it prepares to stop and pick up passengers for Leeds. In this view of Skipton, there are plenty of freight wagons visible, and although by 2022 there had been a great deal of track rationalisation, a good variety of rail freight traffic can still be seen. (Peter Fitton)

This busy scene on 6 March 1965 at Bog Hall crossing, just outside Whitby Station, was not to be repeated. Waiting to leave for York was D259 with its six non-corridor coaches, while LNER 3442 and 62005 on the SLS/MLS *Whitby Moors* railtour would leave at 5.58 pm as the last steam train to Malton. This was the final day of trains along what was later to be re-opened as the North Yorkshire Moors Railway. In those days it was almost deemed normal to stand on the track. (Peter Fitton)

Marston Moor station was opened by the East and West Yorkshire Junction Railway in October 1848, with 'Moor' only added to the name on 1 August 1896. The line from York to Leeds via Harrogate is still open today, but passenger trains stopped calling here on 15 September 1958. A few years later, on 3 October 1964, a dmu has run over the level crossing and is seen passing through the smart looking station on its way to Harrogate. (Peter Fitton)

Another excellent picture of the *Whitby Moors* railtour which would have been a shame to leave out as it shows the imposing Larpool Viaduct at Whitby. This 300-yard long 13 arch brick structure was built in the 1880s, and until 1965 carried the coastal railway to Scarborough. The K4 and K1 engines head the special northbound across the viaduct which will reverse at Prospect Hill Junction to reach Whitby. This involved No. 3442 running round to take the train downhill to Bog Junction. An eight coach dmu can be seen on the Esk Valley line to Middlesbrough. (Peter Fitton)

Having just called at Gargrave to pick up passengers, BR Standard Class 4 No. 75017 restarts for its next call at Hellifield. The train is the 12.22 Saturday Only Leeds City to Morecambe Promenade service which would also call at Lancaster Green Ayre. Based at Skipton when withdrawn in January 1967, the loco saw exactly fifteen years' service after manufacture at Swindon Works. The picture is dated 3rd April 1965. (Peter Fitton)

Newby Wiske was situated on the Leeds Northern line between Ripon and Northallerton. Passing the crossing box, complete with its old NER slotted post lower quadrant signal, Sulzer engined No. D175 is seen hauling a Newcastle to Liverpool express on 10th April 1965. (Peter Fitton)

English Electric Type 4 No. D272 on the 11.00 Newcastle to Liverpool train was photographed crossing the River Ure at Ripon on 23 February 1967. This was just a few days prior to the line being closed to passenger trains although goods workings did continue for a further two years. This route from Harrogate to Northallerton was opened in 1852; in recent years there have been moves to re-open the section to Ripon. (Peter Fitton)

There were two relief *Thames Clyde Express* workings travelling along the Settle-Carlisle line on Maundy Thursday, 23 March 1967. While a very respectable Holbeck Jubilee No. 45647 *Sturdee* worked the northbound train from Leeds, unkempt Kingmoor Britannia No. 70053 *Moray Firth* was in charge of the Up one. Passing through Ribblehead station at speed, it seems the fireman could help very little with sighting! (Peter Fitton)

Wormald Green station was located on the Leeds to Northallerton line and opened in 1848. Closure to passengers came in June 1962, while some goods traffic was still handled until August 1964. The through line north of Harrogate to Northallerton saw the end of passenger trains in March 1967, but on 30 May 1967 Wormald Green had a special visit, when Jubilee No. 45562 *Alberta* arrived with the Royal Train. (Gavin Morrison)

Another view of No. 45562 this time in August 1967 when there were just two 5X Jubilees left in service. On 12 August, it was rostered for the Summer Saturdays Only 10.17 Leeds to Carlisle (06.40 from Birmingham), a duty for which these Holbeck locos were kept. Peter Fitton took this picture of the train passing Bell Busk signal box complete with Midland Railway double telegraph poles still in place.

Cattal station on the York to Harrogate branch line saw this crowded green dmu heading west with an extra working on 31 August 1969. The BR North Eastern Region pale blue posts with their oil lamp heads plus those colourful flower borders certainly made it an attractive place.
(Peter Fitton)

A great atmospheric picture taken at York on 28 October 1971. The star of the show is Deltic D9001 *St. Paddy,* producing a smokescreen as it departs with the 11.00 King's Cross to Newcastle train. Making the picture special are the young enthusiasts, probably on half-term holiday, obviously delighted to see and hear the Deltic in the autumn sunlight. Worth noting is the full trackwork to the engine's left, which includes the middle lines through the station. (John Cooper Smith)

Another Deltic and another terrific image, this time south of York on the ECML at Selby. Commencing on 8 June 1977, the Deltic hauled *Silver Jubilee* express departed King's Cross at 07.46 for Newcastle. Peter Fitton photographed the first northbound run behind No. 55022 *Royal Scots Grey* crossing the Swing Bridge. The sudden appearance of Brush Type 4 No. 47432 on an Up train threatened to spoil the shot, but quick thinking, quicker camera work and possibly a little luck resulted in this never to be repeated picture.

On 13 August 1978 an English Electric Type 4 has stopped at Knaresborough signal box for the handing over of the token to proceed towards York with its special train. The unusual Grade II listed North Eastern signal box (with a Mackenzie and Holland frame) was built on the end of a row of houses in 1873 and later modified to this design. Not obvious in this view, the coaches are on the picturesque viaduct. The crossover enables terminating trains to return to Leeds. (Peter Fitton)

Another scene at Knaresborough, this time dated 20 October 1979. The unusual combination of ex-Midland Railway 4-4-0 No. 1000 and Jubilee Class No. 5690 *Leander* head a special excursion towards York. (Peter Fitton)

On a distinctly murky April morning in 1980, the 07.15 Nottingham to Glasgow is hurrying north at Gargrave towards the Settle and Carlisle line. Peak class locomotives were regularly seen on this service and, checking back through my notes from over forty years ago, No. 45047 is the likely engine appearing through the gloom. (John Matthews)

Saturday 17 May 1980 is remembered as the sunny day when several steam-hauled excursions ran to Manchester in connection with the Liverpool and Manchester 150 celebrations. After No. 6201 *Princess Elizabeth* had reportedly caused lineside fires in the dry weather, and to prevent further ones, these trains were piloted by diesels. This provided the unique sight of ex-works Brush No. 47522 hauling the Midland Compound No. 1000 and its train at Eldroth between Wennington and Settle Junction. (Peter Fitton)

Another victim of the extremely dry weather in May 1980 was this special to Carlisle. The very late running train crosses Gargrave viaduct with Coronation class No. 46229 *Duchess of Hamilton* playing second fiddle behind an unidentified Class 40 diesel. (John Matthews)

While regular steam working through York had been resigned to the history books for some years there was still plenty of interest for the rail enthusiast in May 1981. Pictured left to right on 25 June are No. 46036 on the 16.12 Newcastle-Cardiff, along with light engine No. 47541, the 16.40 Newcastle to King's Cross HST, Deltic No. 55009 *Alycidon* with the 18.14 to King's Cross and a local dmu to Doncaster. (John Matthews)

Towards the end of their twenty-year reign hauling East Coast Main Line expresses, a number of Deltic farewell specials were run. One of these, the *Hadrian Flyer*, was organised by BR, running on 5 December 1981 from Peterborough to Carlisle and can be seen catching the low winter sun on Ribblehead Viaduct. The engine used for the rail tour, that returned via Hexham and York, was No. 55015 (D9015) *Tulyar* presently owned by the Deltic Preservation Society at Barrow Hill. (John Matthews)

Like other seaside resorts, Scarborough station was always a busy place on summer Saturdays. Here on 5 September 1981, No. 08171 is the station pilot whilst now preserved Deltic No. 55002 *The King's Own Yorkshire Light Infantry* waits to leave with the 09.25 train to Newcastle which had arrived as the 08.54 from Filey behind No. 45046. The dmus are working local services to York and Hull. (Peter Fitton)

A little slice of luck as two trains meet at a sunny Bell Busk on 19 February 1983. Heading an Up passenger working from Carlisle to Leeds is No. 40034, while a Leeds to Morecambe dmu service passes on its journey north. Built in September 1959 and initially in service as D234, the loco was named *Accra* in May 1962. (John Matthews)

Here we see No. 40077 at Skipton with the *Thames Clyde Express* special on 24 April 1982. The train organised by T&N Railtours had started out from St. Pancras behind No. 45051 before the Class 40 had taken over at Leeds. At this time, Skipton had two large signal boxes and a host of semaphore signals that were all to disappear when the line to Leeds was electrified in 1994. (John Matthews)

Returning to Bell Busk on 19 February 1983, amazingly within minutes a further scene of passing trains was witnessed, this time looking south at the same location. Approaching the camera is Peak No. 45117 with the *Thames Clyde Express* running from St. Pancras to Glasgow just as No. 40004 rushes into view with a freight for Haverton Hill. Very much a day to remember with the sun as a constant companion. (John Matthews)

For many years, the Trans-Pennine services from Liverpool to York and Scarborough were loco-hauled by a wide variety of motive power. These would vary from the occasional Class 25, Class 47s, Peaks and Deltic locomotives. On 6 June 1983, it was the turn of EE Type 4 No. 40181 to head the 07.05 Liverpool to Scarborough pictured departing York. A short pause under the magnificent station roof allowed the photographer time to dash over the footbridge and capture this image. (John Matthews)

The Hertfordshire Railtours *Norseman 2* special is pictured at Redmire on 18 February 1984, comprising Class 101 dmu cars E53244, E59084, E53149, E53295, E53150, E53188 and E51219. The train visited the Redmire and Eastgate freight-only branch lines before passengers connected on to a locomotive hauled service back to King's Cross. (Paul Shannon)

With a light load
of five coaches in
tow, No. 31440
heads east near
Clapham with the
13.36 Lancaster
to Hull train on
9 June 1984. The
appearance of
Class 31 locos on
these services was
a welcome sight
for both regular
passengers and rail
fans alike, bringing
a touch of variety
to the 'Little' North
Western route from
Settle Junction to
Carnforth.
(Paul Shannon)

The northbound SLOA *Santa Special* on 28 December 1984 is pictured here in the snow approaching Blea Moor signal box while heading for Appleby behind Nos. 40118 and 25080. The train had left Euston behind electric No. 85025, with the Class 40 used between Carnforth and Hellifield. Former SR No. *777 Sir Lamiel* later returned the train to Hellifield whence No. *4472 Flying Scotsman* ran it back to Carnforth for No. 81022 to take over and return to London. At least the steam heating was working on this freezing cold day. (Peter Fitton)

Arriving at Settle station are Nos. 31436 & 31447 with the 16.35 Carlisle-Hull on 17 August 1985. After the withdrawal of the Class 40s the Brush Type 2s were regular locos on Leeds to Carlisle workings, sometimes a single engine would be used, but on longer trains they were often double-headed. (Paul Shannon)

Peak Class No. 45122 was working the 10.53 Scarborough to Holyhead when photographed here at the ex-North Eastern Railway's Malton station on 20 December 1986. The attractive roof over the single remaining platform was unfortunately removed in 1989. The day is remembered as the one when GWR No. 3440 *City of Truro* made two round trips between York and Scarborough. (Peter Fitton)

The reason for the very late running of this Rochdale to Carlisle special soon became apparent when the train finally appeared at Nappa. Having run up the Ribble Valley, the train heads north for Hellifield behind failed loco No. 47709 *Lord Provost* and rescue engine No. 45029. The long wait had been rewarded, as Peaks were quite a rare sight on the line from Blackburn in those days. (John Matthews)

The *Thames Eden Limited* special ran from King's Cross to Carlisle on 21 January 1989. Commencing from London behind electric loco No. 89001, this was removed at Leeds where No. 45106 took over for the run along the Settle to Carlisle line. The Peak is seen here waiting at Skipton before continuing its journey north. (John Matthews)

Two diversions away from the West Coast Main Line converge at Settle Junction on 11 March 1989. To the right, No. 47527 is heading south with the 10.25 Inter-City service from Glasgow Central to London Euston, while waiting on the Carnforth line, to the left, are Nos. 20028 and 20172 and the 6M24 steel coil train from Mossend Yard to Dee Marsh Junction. (Paul Shannon)

This was the scene at Battersby Junction on 6 August 1989 shortly before the closure of the signal box, removal of the semaphores and track changes. Pacer No. 142519 is departing for Middlesbrough, whilst Nos.142516 and 143619 await reversal for Whitby. The two GW livery Pacers had recently arrived from Plymouth and for a while were given 5XX numbers. Originally named Ingleby Junction from its 1858 opening on the Picton to Grosmont line, it was renamed in 1878. Since closure west of here in the 1950s, Battersby has continued as a reversing point on this single track Esk Valley branch line. The water tank (which that day contained fish!) and the crane survive, but just one platform is now in use, plus a run-round loop. (Peter Fitton)

Railway photography doesn't get much better than this image taken at Blea Moor on 21 December 1996. Running north on the *Christmas Cumbrian Mountain Express* is LMS Stanier Mogul No. 2968 complete with a Black Five tender. Enough said, I think. (John Cooper Smith)

The Hertfordshire Railtours *Rylestone Cowboy* began its journey north from King's Cross at 07.29 on 21 March 1998. Leading the special was No. 56114 which ran along the ECML before making its way to Skipton station. On arrival, the tour had around a 30-minute break before continuing with a short run north to North Junction where No. 37685 (previously on the rear) would take the special along the branch line to Rylestone. The EE Type 3 can be seen along the branch shortly after leaving Skipton. (John Matthews)

A modern-day picture that seems to be almost timeless. A truly great image of A4 No. 60009 *Union of South Africa* on a test run near Clapham in April 2017. The train set out from Carnforth and would return there after running via Hellifield, Blackburn and Preston. (John Cooper Smith)

CUMBRIA

Cumbria is the third largest county in England having only two major urban areas, Barrow-in-Furness in the south and the county town Carlisle at the very north. The county is mainly rural and contains the Lake District National Park which attracts a multitude of visitors, ramblers and motor cars every year. It is also a very mountainous region, Scaffell Pike at 3,209 feet being the highest peak in England. Cutting through Cumbria is the West Coast Main line, while at a much slower and more relaxing pace the Cumbrian Coast line winds its way from Barrow to Carlisle, with the Irish Sea to keep the traveller company. It should also be noted that much of the Settle to Carlisle line is also in Cumbria.

We start our journey around Cumbria at the classic location of Ais Gill, seen here on 8 July 1961. Pictured close to the county boundary with North Yorkshire a welcome hint of sunshine appears as Jubilee No. 45640 *Frobisher* rushes south with the Up relief, *Thames Clyde Express*. Built at Crewe in 1934, the Stanier 4-6-0 was in service for nearly thirty years before being withdrawn from Kingmoor shed in March 1964. (Peter Fitton)

High in the northern Pennines on the border between Cumbria and North Yorkshire, BR Standard Class 4 No. 76021 passes the signal box at Stainmore Summit on 5 August 1961. The six-coach train in tow is the Saturdays Only working from Blackpool to Newcastle. The line was built by the South Durham & Lancashire Union Railway and opened in 1861 linking Bishop Auckland and Tebay. Construction took four years, the line cutting through the wild landscape and climbing steep gradients that required the building of twelve viaducts. The line was closed as a through route on 22 January 1962. (Gavin Morrison)

The SLS/MLS *Furness Rail Tour* pauses at Coniston during its tour of Barrow and South Lakeland railways on 27 August 1961. Originating from Lancaster Castle station behind No. 43282, the train visited Dalton, Ramsden Dock and Millom before Royal Scot No. 46152 *The King's Dragoon Guardsman* returned the special from Morecambe to Manchester Victoria. Although these two locos were used on the tour, Class 4F No. 44347 took on the bulk of the work and is seen here taking a short rest before continuing to Morecambe. (Ken Roberts)

A busy scene at Carlisle Station as the St. Pancras to Edinburgh service *The Waverley* slows to pick up passengers for Scotland. Stops would be made at Hawick, St. Boswells, Melrose and Galashiels on the 98-mile journey to Edinburgh. At the head of the train is Peak No. D30, later to be renumbered 45029, a number it retained until becoming No. 97410 a year prior to withdrawal in August 1988. (John S. Whiteley)

A wide view looking south at Carlisle on 13 April 1963 as No. D373 arrives with the London Euston to Glasgow Central *Royal Scot*. Complete with headboard, the Camden loco (later to be No. 40173) looks in fine fettle without its small yellow nose panel as it approaches under the slightly threatening sky. (John S. Whiteley)

Grange-over-Sands station appears today virtually the same as when this photograph was taken on 29 July 1963. Obviously, the mode of transport has changed dramatically, and while today modern diesel units operate along the line to Barrow-in-Furness, in the early 1960s steam traction was still very much the order of the day. On this particular sunny afternoon, Stanier 2-6-4T loco No. 42594 slows for day trippers on a Barrow-Morecambe service. (Peter Fitton)

Track workers and fishermen can be seen in this picture taken from the train at Greenodd as it runs along the single line Lakeside Branch on 1 September 1963. Horwich built Stanier Black 5 No. 44982 is leading the service that ran Monday to Friday from Blackpool. After closure, the bridge was replaced and the track bed became a main road. (Peter Fitton)

An evening shot at Carlisle, in fact taken at 7.30pm on 28 March 1964. Arrived at platform 4 is a stopping train from Edinburgh having worked south along the Waverley route. Motive power on this occasion was provided by No. D5301, this had been built by the Birmingham Railway Carriage and Wagon Company in 1958. Under the TOPS numbering system, the loco became 26001 and is presently awaiting overhaul at the Caledonian Railway (Brechin). (John S. Whiteley)

On Easter Sunday 1964, Upperby allocated Royal Scot loco No. 46118 *Royal Welch Fusilier* departs Carlisle in grand style after pausing to pick up passengers on the 09.30 Manchester Victoria-Glasgow service. Although No. 46118 looks to be in good shape, the writing was on the wall and it was taken out of service less than three months later, on 13 June 1964. (John S. Whiteley)

Starting out from Kirkby Stephen West on 6 June 1964 is the mid-day train from Hellifield to Carlisle. Hauled by Sulzer Type 2 No. D7581, it would call at all stations along the Settle to Carlisle line, completing the seventy-seven miles in just under two and a half hours. Allocated new to Nottingham 16A on 28 December 1963, the loco soon found itself transferred to Carlisle for crew training. Running as No. 25231 from April 1974 it spent some time in Scotland before being stored at Basford Hall in 1985. (Peter Fitton)

On 13 June 1964, the West Riding Branch of the RCTS organised the *Solway Ranger* from Leeds City to Carlisle. At Penrith, a pair of Ivatt 2-6-0s took over the special from Merchant Navy Class No. 35012 *United States Line* for the forty-mile cross-country run to Workington. At Bassenthwaite Lake, Nos. 46426 and 46458 enjoyed a five-minute break prior to continuing westbound towards Cockermouth. Both Ivatt locos were in service for a few more years, both being withdrawn by the end of 1966. (Gavin Morrison)

Fast forward about four hours, and the *Solway Ranger* is now departing Carlisle for Silloth with two very different engines in the form of GNSR No. 49 *Gordon Highlander* and Caledonian Railway No. 123; both incidentally can still be seen as static exhibits in Scottish railway museums. The railways to Port Carlisle and Silloth had a long and somewhat complicated history after their first opening in 1854, but all services ceased when the line closed on 7 September 1964. (Peter Fitton)

Travelling on a Liverpool Exchange to Windermere train behind Class 5 No. 45376, we encounter Stanier tank No. 42680 waiting just outside Oxenholme with an Up service. With only one line here for branch line trains, delays were likely. The mixed coaching stock was typical of the day, 31 July 1964. Note the starter signal, which was north of the station on the main line; some trains waited here for banking assistance to Grayrigg. (Peter Fitton)

Rebuilt Patriot No. 45527 *Southport* is seen hauling the 1M25 Glasgow to Euston express through Shap station on a very wet 18 July 1964. The station opened from December 1846 until closure in July 1968, although by 1964, the awning over the low northbound platform was showing its age. Paraffin lamps were still in use until closure. Notice also the original footbridge and that the track on this main line was still using bullhead rails. (Peter Fitton)

A total of just ten BR Class 6 Clan locomotives were built at Crewe in 1952 mainly for use on the Scottish Region. Many of the class were in operation for a little over ten years. About to leave Carlisle on 11 August 1964 is No. 72007 *Clan Mackintosh* with the 09.10 to Glasgow. This loco had a slightly longer life, running for thirteen years, before being withdrawn from its only allocated shed at Kingmoor. (John S. Whiteley)

Opened by the Furness Railway in 1869, the railway from Ulverston to Lakeside had a regular passenger service with connections for boat crossings to Windermere. During the summer months, numerous excursions from the North-West would also arrive, bringing in welcome sightseers and ramblers. In this wide view of Lakeside on 28 August 1964 a pair of Stanier Black 5 locos Nos. 44730 and 44877 are pictured along with signals and buildings all very much in place, considering closure was just a year away. (Gavin Morrison)

Windermere station in 1964 was still a busy place, with several platforms in use, plus a coal siding and a cattle dock. Four sets of coaches can be seen in this photograph taken on 30 August as Class 5 No. 44692 waits to leave with the 2.50pm all-stations to Oxenholme. Sadly, today there is only a single platform without a run-round loop, a supermarket occupying much of the site and a limited train service. (Peter Fitton)

At Scout Green No. 70006 *Robert Burns* is climbing Shap with a Euston-Glasgow relief working on 31 July 1966. Built at Crewe in April 1951, the Britannia Class 7P6F 4-6-2 was a long-time resident at Kingmoor shed from where it was withdrawn in May 1967. (John Cooper Smith)

The Furness Railway Lakeside branch line is again the subject of this picture taken on 5 September 1965, the final day of regular passenger trains. At Plumpton Junction that day, 10A Carnforth's No. 44892 is heading the Summer Only train from Blackpool which will stop at Ulverston where the engine will run-round. The single line tablet post is visible on the left where the branch tracks turned off; veering sharply to the right is the Bardsea Branch, by this time only serving the Glaxo factory. After a brake van special in September 1967 and movement of stock to Haverthwaite for the future Lakeside Railway, the branch track here was removed. The attractive signal box closed in March 2000 along with the sidings, leaving just plain double track today. (Peter Fitton)

At Scout Green again but looking in the opposite direction, No. 70012 *John of Gaunt* is coming down Shap heading a Glasgow-Morecambe empty stock train. In service for sixteen years, No. 70012 continued to run until the last day of 1967. (John Cooper Smith)

No words are needed to describe this master shot taken by Gerry Dixon, other than No.45562 is pictured at Dillicar on 25 February 1967.

Making its way along the Lune Gorge is Stanier 4-6-0 No. 45072 with a train of holidaymakers from Glasgow to Blackpool on 22 July 1967. At Preston, the train may well have run via the East Lancs and Farington Curve lines to avoid stopping in the busy station. Perhaps it was the excellent light shining on No. 45072 that made it appear to be in great shape, but time was running out and sadly two months later it was withdrawn from Carnforth shed. (John Cooper Smith)

A few similarities with the previous photo in that we have a Black 5 on the same day taken by the same photographer. The differences are worth seeing though as No. 44674 hurries through the site of Grayrigg station with a northbound Morecambe to Glasgow Saturday Only working. The buildings and cabin behind the train look in reasonable condition considering the last passenger train called on 1 February 1954. Coming out of Horwich Works on 31 March 1950, this long-time resident of Kingmoor shed was cut up on 31 March 1968, not a happy eighteenth birthday! (John Cooper Smith)

In the Lune Valley, No. 70022, the 'real' Tornado, is seen heading south at the head of a Glasgow to Blackpool train on 22 July 1967. These direct trains from Scotland to Blackpool North continued to run well into the 1980s, but today a change of train at Preston is needed to complete the journey. (John Cooper Smith)

Each summer there was a special train from London Euston to Keswick for the Convention there. On a sunny 22 July 1967, D313 was piloting Ivatt Class 4 No. 43139 with the return train when seen running wrong line near Troutbeck. The diesel would run round at Penrith and take the train on southwards; two locos were needed for shunting and the gradients. Previous years had seen two Moguls on the branch with another larger engine from Penrith. Only one line was being used as an economy; unfortunately, the line closed in March 1972. (Peter Fitton)

With the Howgills as a backdrop, Britannia 4-6-2 No. 70004 (formerly *William Shakespeare*) makes an impressive sight as it heads south at Grayrigg with the 08.30 Carlisle to Birmingham express in July 1967. Once the pride of Stewarts Lane MPD, it was a regular performer on the luxury boat train the *Golden Arrow*. In less glamorous times, the Pacific loco appears here with a makeshift number plate and fixing bolts for the 'arrow' that was probably removed sometime before its move north to Kingmoor via Crewe North shed. Of interest may be the superb oil painting by Terence Cuneo portraying No. 70004 and the *Golden Arrow* arriving at Dover. (John Cooper Smith)

Derby Lightweight diesel units were still used on many services during the 1960s in what is now called Cumbria. Here, two sets, the leading one in BR blue, are seen passing Milnthorpe station with a Windermere to Carnforth service on 8 August 1967. With its gas lamps, wooden shelter and cast iron supported footbridge on the low main line platform, the station was in near-original condition. Closure came not long afterwards. (Peter Fitton)

On the short list for the cover of the book was this superb view at Plumpton, dated 4 November 1967. In the excellent morning light, Brush loco No. D1853 rushes past with a Carlisle-Euston express, while waiting in the Up goods loop is Stanier Black Five No. 45013 on a Carlisle Yard to Banbury goods working. Plumpton did in fact have its own station but that saw early closure in May 1948.

A great view of the southern end of Carlisle station on 4 June 1970. A pair of Class 50 locos Nos. 447 and 429 depart with the 14.00 Glasgow-Euston service. The line to Maryport is curving out of shot on the left-hand side, while Bog Junction freight line is in the cutting under the second coach. A total of fifty of these locos were built, principally to work trains from Crewe to Scotland, but when the WCML was electrified north of Crewe in 1974 all the class was transferred to the Western Region. (John Cooper Smith)

Approaching Scout Green on 29 May 1971 is a Euston to Glasgow express hauled by another set of English Electric Class 50s. Running without nameplates at the time, Nos. 431 and 422 would later appear as 50031 *Hood* and 50022 *Anson* respectively. The photographer recalls that the noise from the oncoming locos sounded 'almost as good as steam', a good wake up call after a night spent in your nearby tent. (Les Nixon)

The peace of a sunny Penrith summer's day is disturbed by the sound of EE Type 4 No. 221 accelerating away from the station with the 12.00 Carlisle to Preston service. On arrival there, it would be attached to the 12.56 from Blackpool North and then continue to London Euston. In this view, dated 27 July 1971, little had changed since the end of steam in 1967, but electrification was on its way. (Peter Fitton)

During the Penmanshiel Tunnel closure diversions, trains south of Edinburgh were diverted via Beattock, Carlisle and Hexham to reach Newcastle. On Saturday 28 July 1979, Peter Fitton photographed HST 254027 on a service to King's Cross passing the delightful Denton School crossing on the Newcastle to Carlisle line. The cloudy bright lighting and clean coaches have helped to produce a fine record of that day; the scene is much changed today.

On 25 April 1981, a sunny Dentdale was blanketed in snow, with some roads blocked, but as Deltic No. 55002 was due northbound on a rail tour from York, it seemed worthwhile to be there. Unfortunately, it was not realised on the day that this train was being diverted via Carnforth and Shap! The first northbound train was running 150 minutes late, but the 1S68 Nottingham-Glasgow Central express, here seen crossing the 11-arch Arten Gill viaduct, was running almost on time. (Peter Fitton)

This was normally a job for a Class 47 loco; therefore, it was quite a surprise when No. 25097 turned up on the 10.16 Barrow-in-Furness to Nottingham train on 12 July 1983. Arriving at Dalton, the former Furness Railway station, the train has just emerged from the 225-yard Dalton Tunnel. The distant signal is for Dalton Junction, where the Barrow loop diverges from the short section of line through to Park South Junction. (Paul Shannon)

Sadly, during recent times the cancelling of a train has almost become commonplace, mainly due possibly to the lack of spare resources i.e., engines and coaches or even 'no available train crew'. Also, the ingenuity and the 'must keep the trains running' attitude seems to be a thing of the past. Wind back to around 1998 at Preston, and a Glasgow to Penzance train is fifteen minutes away from its engine change from electric to diesel. The problem being there was no diesel loco to be found, so head of control Dave, nicknamed 'The Eagle', scratched his head and located the Carlisle to Preston route-learner light engine twenty minutes away at Daisyfield, Blackburn. Wheels were set in motion and it wasn't long before the route learner Deltic No. 55022 *Royal Scots Grey* was hooked up to the Penzanze service taking it as far as Stockport, though some say through to Crewe. Great stuff. A less glamorous rescue, but from a passenger's view just as important, can be seen here as No. 25058 tows the failed 09.20 Lancaster-Carlisle dmu at Seascale on 22 August 1985. (John Matthews)

Incongruously painted in Railfreight Distribution livery, No. 90047 passes a wintry Greenholme with the 08.45 London Euston to Glasgow Central train on 9 February 1991. In 2022, the loco can still be seen in operation working intermodal trains for Freightliner. (Paul Shannon)

The 17 August 1991 *Cumbrian Coast Express* from London Euston to Workington began its 600-mile round trip behind AC electric traction as far as Carnforth, where No. 46203 *Princess Margaret Rose* took over. After a break of an hour at Workington, No. 4472 Flying *Scotsman* was hooked on to the train for the southbound leg of the tour back to Carnforth. The spotless engine, coaches and signals make for a great picture as the train approaches Whitehaven Bransty. (John Cooper Smith)

Had the news travelled down the grapevine or were the onlookers just taking a pleasant stroll along the bank of the River Kent at Arnside. Either way, they had the pleasure of seeing two Class 20 locos, Nos. 20059 and 20168, crossing the viaduct and then slowing for the next stop at Arnside station. This was very rare motive power for Furness line trains, although loco-hauled services still ran up until recently in the shape of Class 37/4s. Pictured on the 25 April 1992, the six coach 15.32 Barrow to Preston catches the afternoon sun as it heads east. (Peter Fitton)

An extremely early alarm call was needed to catch the *Coronation Scot* special on 27 September 2003. Departing Manchester Victoria at 05.02 behind Brush No. 47854, the train ran via Bolton to Carnforth where No. 6233 *Duchess of Sutherland* took over for the run over Shap to Carlisle. The special, complete with *Royal Scot* headboard, is pictured at Greenholme at sunrise. With a little imagination and a longing for the past, you could think it was a very late running Anglo-Scottish sleeper train, often hauled by Coronation Class locomotives sometime in the early 1960s. (John Cooper Smith)

Situated in the Lune Gorge south of Tebay is Dillicar. At this classic location, about half a mile south of Tebay troughs, Princess Royal Class No. 6201 *Princess Elizabeth* is taking a run at Shap but not slowing for a banker today! The train is the northbound *Cumbrian Mountain Express* for Carlisle, producing an impressive sight on 30 July 2011. (John Cooper Smith)

Against the splendid backdrop of St. Bees Head, Royal Scot Class No. 46115 *Scots Guardsman* is heading south with the *Winter Cumbrian Coast Express* on 23 March 2017. Arriving at Carnforth behind electric No. 86259, the steam engine was soon attached and the train continued along the WCML to Carlisle. After reversal and a short stay, No. 46115 worked south through Workington and Barrow before being replaced by electric traction at Carnforth. (John Cooper Smith)

Picking up passengers at Appleby on 18 August 2004 is the 09.47 Leeds-Carlisle train. Surprisingly, problems with two of the three regular EWS Class 37/4 locos meant a welcome outing along the Settle-Carlisle line for Mainline liveried No. 37372. Built in June 1963, it was first allocated to Cardiff Canton as No. D6859. Worth noting is the 37 was over forty years old at this time, and still giving excellent service. (John Matthews)

In 2015, Arriva were awarded the contract to run the 'Northern' rail franchise. Things didn't go well with the new company, and it wasn't long before the wheels started to come off, literally. After the introduction of their new timetable in 2018, the whole network went into virtual meltdown. Shortage of drivers, cancellations, no rolling stock, late running and more cancellations led ultimately to the company being relieved of its franchise and leaving 'Northern' in effect 'nationalised'. One line hit particularly hard by the chaos was the one from Oxenholme to Windermere, when some days just a replacement bus or two would be in use. Behind the scenes much work was being done by politicians, railway people, businessmen and others to get the trains back on the tracks. The solution came in the shape of Carnforth-based West Coast Railway Company, who provided various locos and coaches to allow a regular passenger service to commence. At Windermere on 24 June 2018, No. 33029 is about to leave with the 13.20 to Oxenholme. (John Matthews)

Situated in the Lake District is the village of Salterwhaite, where this great photo of Merchant Navy No. 35018 *British India Line* was taken on 9 December 2018. The train was a *Santa Special* from Carnforth to Carlisle run by the West Coast Railway Company with the loco working hard climbing Shap. The former Southern Railway engine, built at Eastleigh in 1945, was withdrawn in August 1964, and after fifteen years at Woodham's scrapyard, it was rescued and work to return it to its former glory started. The restoration of the engine started off slowly and it wasn't until moving to Carnforth in 2012 that it returned to main line working order. (John Cooper Smith)

A big round of applause for the now publicly owned London North Eastern Railway for bucking the trend of bus replacement agony. While Avanti, Northern and many more opt for the easy way out by dusting off a few old buses and joining the next five-mile queue of traffic, LNER recently took the trouble to run a timetable of diverted trains from Scotland to London. Over a number of weekends during autumn 2021, the bright shiny Azuma trains could be seen along the Tyne Valley Line and at Carlisle station, where on 25 September No. 800104 prepares to depart with a train for King's Cross. At the same time, No. 57313 arrives on a Northern Belle *S&C Steam Special*, unfortunately without the steam due to the failure of No. 6201 *Princess Elizabeth*! Incidentally similar ECML diversions took place again in late 2022. (John Matthews)

NORTH-EAST

The North-East of England has four counties in the region, County Durham, Tyne and Wear, Northumberland and a part of North Yorkshire. The industrial history of the area consisted of coal mining, steel making, chemicals, shipbuilding and salt making that have unfortunately all declined in recent times. The North-East though is bouncing back from the closures of the old industries, and new businesses are now developing in bioscience, computing, electronics, renewable energy along with the Nissan car factory at Sunderland. Running through the region is the ECML from London to Edinburgh which calls at Newcastle, Durham and Darlington. In addition, there is the picturesque Tyne Valley Line to Carlisle via Hexham and the extensive Tyne and Wear Metro light rail system.

The joint SLS/MLS *Ashington Rail Tour* was run on 10 June 1967. Starting out from Huddersfield behind Black Five No. 45428, the special made its way to York where Jubilee No. 45562 *Alberta* took over for the journey north to Ashington NCB. At the colliery, NCB No. 39 ran a number of trips between Lynmouth and back carrying passengers in three Furness/LNER heritage coaches. (John S. Whiteley)

Constructed between 1847 and 1850, the Royal Border Bridge was designed by Robert Stephenson for the York, Newcastle and Berwick Railway. The stone-built Grade I listed viaduct is 659 metres long and has 28 spans carrying it across the River Tweed. In this dramatic picture, Deltic No. 55006 *The Fife & Forfar Yeomanry* can be seen with the 16.00 King's Cross to Edinburgh service on 12 June 1976. Some eagle-eyed readers may be able to pick out the boating activities on the river below, it's amazing what some people will do to try and get that special master shot. (John Cooper Smith)

Crossing the impressive Durham Viaduct on 29 July 1978 is the 09.00 Edinburgh to King's Cross train. The last Deltic to be built, No. 55021 *Argyll & Sutherland Highlander,* is seen running high above the neat terraced houses, a long wheelbase transit van and a row of cars lining the steep climb. (Peter Fitton)

Nearing the site of the former Scremerston station, closed in 1951, is Brush Type 4 No. 47539 running northbound with the 13.20 Newcastle to Berwick on 29 May 1979. At the time, trains were operating between the two stations following the collapse of Penmanshiel Tunnel on 17 March 1979 and before the new alignment had been completed allowing trains to run through from Newcastle to Edinburgh. (John S. Whiteley)

Saltburn station, located at the eastern end of the Tees Valley Line from Bishop Auckland, was opened in August 1861 by the Stockton and Darlington Railway. On 18 December 1979, a Class 101 dmu prepares to depart the rather run-down station for Darlington. Saltburn today has a service of two trains per hour from its bay platforms, and while the white ornate station buildings are still in place, they are now in private hands. (Gavin Morrison)

Exactly a year before its withdrawal, Peak diesel No. 45025 was still in main line use. Photographed here hauling the 11.20 Newcastle-Liverpool express past Hett Mill signal box along the ECML south of Durham on a sunny 16 May 1980. When new to the rails in 1961, the Sulzer powered loco was numbered D19. (Peter Fitton)

It was appropriate that LMS Class 5 No. 4767 was able to work some special trains to celebrate the 200th anniversary of George Stephenson's birth at Wylam on 9 June 1781. The 18.45 train from Newcastle to Hexham is seen near Wylam in perfect light on 6 June 1981. Unique amongst the 842 Class 5s that were built, No. 44767, as it was later numbered, featured outside Stephenson link motion, an experimental double chimney and Timken roller bearings. Presently residing at Carnforth, it actually never carried the name *George Stephenson* while working on BR. (Peter Fitton)

Pictured at a favourite spot for rail photographers, Deltic No. 55007 *Pinza* heads a Carlisle to Edinburgh local train at Stella in the Tyne Valley. There were two coal fired power stations here, aptly named Stella North and Stella South, sitting either side of the River Tyne. Coal trains ran on both sides of the river to supply the stations that closed in 1991 after nearly forty years of operation. (Peter Fitton)

With Gateshead in the background, Deltic No. 55010 *The King's Own Scottish Borderer* is photographed crossing the King Edward VII Bridge on the approach to Newcastle station. The train is the 09.40 King's Cross to Edinburgh service seen on 18 September 1981 as the end of the Deltic era draws ever nearer. (Peter Fitton)

If you are looking for a railway image with lots of atmosphere, then look no further. In this dramatic shot, the train, the light and the smoke all come together to make a truly special picture. Heading south over Durham Viaduct on 16 October 1981 is a King's Cross bound HST complete with power cars Nos. 43097 and 43058.

(Paul Shannon)

With the South Bank Coke Works as the backdrop, a Metropolitan Cammell dmu arrives at the station's island platform with a Saltburn to Darlington service on 20 March 1982. The station was closed on 23 July 1984 and replaced by a more convenient one 700 yards further east.

(Paul Shannon)

With the temperature well below zero, a Class 47 sits at the head of a short train at Newcastle in early 1982. Although regular steam trains had left the railway scene many years before, one could almost be forgiven for thinking they were still very much alive. (John Matthews)

Towards the end of their life on BR, the Class 46s were concentrated at Gateshead, previously also being allocated to Bristol and Laira Plymouth for a number of years. On the bright morning of 21 April 1982, No. 46031 catches the sun as it prepares to depart Newcastle with the 08.10 for Edinburgh. Right up to their final withdrawal in 1984, the remaining locos were kept busy on freight workings and Summer Saturday trains, typically the Newcastle and York to Blackpool North services. (John Matthews)

Still at Newcastle, Brush Type 2 No. 31409 prepares to leave on a morning service to Scarborough alongside long time Gateshead loco No. 47416. Around this time, in the early 1980s, Gateshead MPD had a very large allocation of diesels, including classes 31, 37, 40, 46, 47 and 55s. (John Matthews)

Everything appears to be in good order at Haltwhistle on 16 July 1984 with a fine set of signals, distinctive signal box and attractive station buildings. Completing the picture is a Metro Cammell dmu waiting to depart on the 10.43 Carlisle to Newcastle train. Up until May 1976, Haltwhistle was the terminus for the 13-mile branch line that ran north from Alston. (Paul Shannon)

Departing Haltwhistle after a stop for water is the *Northern Belle* excursion to Carlisle. The special started out from King's Cross with No. 47402 taking the train north along the ECML before Coronation Class No. 46229 *Duchess of Hamilton* took over at Eaglescliffe. The train would reverse at Carlisle, with a little assistance from shunt loco No. 08911, prior to returning home via Petteril Bridge Junction and Settle. The scene was photographed on 16 March 1985.

(John Cooper Smith)

The delightful station at Hexham saw Brush Sulzer No. 47527 employed on several stopping trains along the Newcastle and Carlisle line on 5 September 1988. Here, passengers prepare to board the 12.37 from Carlisle. This now Grade II listed station is one of the oldest in the world, dating from 1835, and until recently had goods yard buildings and stables, but no longer in use. First numbered D1110, No. 47527 was withdrawn from service in November 1992 and scrapped in South Wales. (Peter Fitton)

Situated on the Bishop Auckland to Darlington branch line is the small station of Heighington. On 9 April 2011, West Coast Railway Company Class 47 No. 47804, with No. 47786 on the rear, are returning to Norwich with the *York & Weardale Rambler* special. Organised by NENTA, the train has travelled down the Weardale Railway that had seen its last goods train from Eastgate in 1992. Passenger services resumed in May 2010 and a year later the line saw coal trains running from Wolsingham to Scunthorpe. (Brian Sherrington)

No apologies for a quick look back at the Royal Border Bridge here on 9 May 2019, and although electrification has appeared, it takes nothing away from the stunning view of the viaduct that crosses the River Tweed. On Day 1 of the *Highlands and Islands Explorer* tour, the slightly unusual pairing of A3 No. 60103 *Flying Scotsman* and B1 No. 61306 *Mayflower* make a great picture as they haul their long train north to Edinburgh. (John Cooper Smith)

Running through Haydon Bridge, on the Carlisle to Newcastle line, No. 67029 *Royal Diamond* is pictured heading the diverted 08.24 Edinburgh to King's Cross service. Immediately behind the diesel is Virgin East Coast electric loco No. 91125 which would later take over the train on its journey south to London. (Martin Hilbert)